REINVENT ME

HOW TO TRANSFORM YOUR LIFE AND CAREER

WATKINS

Sharing Wisdom Since
1893

This edition first published in the UK and USA 2017 by

Watkins, an imprint of Watkins Media Limited

19 Cecil Court

London WC2N 4EZ

enquiries@watkinspublishing.com

Design and typography copyright © Watkins Media Limited 2017

Text copyright © Camilla Sacre-Dallerup 2017

1 3 5 7 9 10 8 6 4 2

Designed and typeset by Gail Jones

Printed and bound in the United Kingdom

A CIP record for this book is available from the British Library

ISBN: 978-1-78678-060-7

www.watkinspublishing.com

Contents

Acknowledgements

It is with such gratitude in my heart that I write these acknowledgements. Before I set out on this journey, I had meditated on the fact that I wanted writing this book to be a joyful, rather than stressful, experience. To make that possible I knew I needed a great editor, who would also be my team-mate and help me stick to my deadlines. This person came in the shape of a wonderful lady called Dawn Bates. Dawn, you know how I feel about you, but I want everyone to know. I could have not asked for a better team-mate. Thank you for being so fabulous and easy to work with it – I have loved every bit of working with you and I felt that you were just as passionate about creating a book that can help and heal as I was. Thank you from the bottom of my heart.

Thank you to the equally amazing commissioning editor Jo Lal, who once again believed in my vision and allowed me creative freedom to bring it to life, but who equally gave such honest and helpful advice. I love being on this journey with Watkins and with you.

And, of course, the deepest thank you to my husband, Kevin, who sat up late with me brainstorming when this idea came about, and who supported and believed in me all the way to the finish line. Thank you for your love and support, and for reminding me daily to enjoy life as well as work hard.

Thank you to all those people who shared their reinvention stories throughout this book – I know that what you achieved will inspire and encourage others to do the same.

It is my dream for this book to be translated into Danish, so that my parents can read this acknowledgement without me translating it: thank you for always being there for me and for reminding me every day that we can achieve whatever we put our minds to. I love you both so much and your support means the world to me. And to my sister, Jeanet, for always giving me sound and down-to-earth advice and always having my back – thank you, I love you!

I would probably not have even imagined writing my own book without the extraordinary people who went before me, and who were so very honest about their journey as a writer: Wayne Dyer, Marianne Williamson and Oprah Winfrey, thank you for your inspiration.

'When I let go of what I am,

I become what I might be.'

Lao Tzu

Introduction

Congratulations! By opening this book, you've just taken the first step toward reinventing your life – and I'm so excited for you. As you work through the Reinvent Me programme, be prepared for an exciting, interactive experience!

I've successfully reinvented my life and career in more ways than one and I've written this book to share the tools I used. I'm passionate about helping people to find the courage within to fulfil their dreams. I know more than anyone that reinvention is not an overnight job – it takes courage, perseverance and hard work, but by following my reinvention programme, the journey will be that bit easier for you. By doing the exercises in each chapter, you will gradually take steps toward achieving your goal and grow in confidence as you see your reinvention come to fruition.

For those of you who aren't aware of my background, I was a champion professional dancer before becoming one of the original cast members of one of Britain's most successful TV shows, *Strictly Come Dancing*, a global phenomenon which went on to become known as *Dancing with the Stars* worldwide. In 2008, my sixth series, I achieved my dream of winning the show with my celebrity partner Tom Chambers, but then made the controversial decision to quit. And this is where my reinvention really began. Performing and being a 'celebrity' had its perks, but it was no longer rewarding in itself and I wasn't as happy and contented as I knew I could be.

I wanted to fulfil my dream of moving to Los Angeles and, having completed my training in 2009, become a Life Coach and hypnotherapist. I had used these tools throughout my life in sports and TV to achieve my goals, and I had reached a place where I felt passionate about using them to help other people. I was also seeking who I really was, so my reinvention was as much a personal journey as it was a major career change.

I am now a successful Life and Mindful Living Coach and a certified hypnotherapist, with clients from all over the world in my Los Angeles and London clinics. I have used the programme of exercises in this book personally and with many clients, both one-to-one and in workshops. I know from personal experience the power of the exercises and how effective they are in helping people to find what they truly want in life.

I have been fortunate to work with many clients from all walks of life, including many celebrities, and have successfully helped them to make major positive life changes. I have lifted many trophies throughout my career, but nothing beats the feeling of empowering someone else and watching that person ignite their power and confidence and step into their light. That to me is truly magical and what life is all about. That is why I wanted to write this book, so that you, the reader, could step into your own power and connect with the beauty and creativity you have inside of you.

Nowadays, it has become acceptable to reinvent ourselves – unlike earlier generations, we are no longer expected to accept our situation. In fact, people are expected to move with the times, to grow and to learn to keep up with an ever-changing world. People very rarely stay in a job for life and many move on if a relationship is making them unhappy. It's common for people to talk about their 'journey' as they go through different experiences – both good and bad – and grow and change. Even though this freer approach to life opens up more opportunities, it also involves us taking more risks and sometimes making difficult decisions. Although it's widely much more acceptable to change course, we can still meet resistance from ourselves and others, which is why it helps to follow a programme and use effective self-help tools, or work with a Life Coach.

What does reinvention mean to you?

Perhaps you want to make a big life change, such as start a new career, relocate or start or end a relationship. Or you might want to make small changes within – perhaps find new hobbies and interests – to challenge you and help you live a more contented and fulfilled life. Perhaps you don't know yet what you want to reinvent – you just know that you want something to change – and that's fine too. As you read through this book and do the exercises, you will come to discover what reinvention means to you.

As a Life Coach I've worked with clients on many different types of reinvention – parents who have been at home raising children, then lacked confidence to return to the workplace; clients who have worked their whole lives in a profession and then suddenly had no drive or passion for it at all; people who are unhappy in a relationship, but are fearful of letting it go. But behind all these practical changes, there is often a deeper reinvention. As you start to make life changes, you will peel back the layers to discover who you really are. You may not, in fact, be reinventing yourself, but actually uncovering the real you that was there all along. This has certainly been my experience.

When you reinvent your life, whether personally or professionally, other changes may follow, creating a snowball effect and opening up opportunities in different areas of your life. In the midst of chaos, these opportunities can be missed so it's important to raise your awareness and identify them when they present themselves. Instead of being stressed and frustrated, you will start attracting different connections and people into your life because you have created time to observe and perceive situations differently. It really is true that 'the change starts with you' – small but conscious changes you make every day can affect your life in more ways than you may be able to imagine now.

One barrier to change might be your own attitude. When you think of your goal, do you find yourself making negative statements? 'I'm too old to learn that.' 'I don't have the talent for that.' 'I'm not creative enough for that.' 'I live too far away to be able to do that,' and so on. Start to become aware of how you speak about yourself when you're thinking about your goal. Having the right attitude and self-belief is key to your reinvention, and I promise that as you work through this programme it will leave you feeling much more positive about yourself and the changes you want to make.

About this programme
Making any sort of change can be overwhelming in the beginning, so I've divided the REINVENT programme into eight clear, achievable parts that you can do at your own pace. Consider this book as a friend who gently reminds you to take steps of action toward achieving your goal. At each stage, I encourage you to connect with your intuition and allow it to guide you. Be brave and honest with yourself as you do the exercises – this will help you get to the bottom of the changes you need to make to ultimately unravel your true self, and get on the right path toward your reinvention.

Before we get started, let me explain how to work your way through the programme. Each of the letters of REINVENT represents a part of the programme from '**1. Recognize**' the need to change to '**8. Transformation**', as you turn your dream into a reality. I recommend reading the entire book and committing to the exercises if you want to get the full benefits.

REINVENT

RECOGNIZE: Work out where you are at and where you need to go.

EGO: Learn how to free yourself from ego-based decisions.

INNOVATION: Plan what action you need to take to start turning your dream into a reality.

NOW: Stop procrastinating and start taking action!

VISUALIZE: Visualize your reinvented life and find the courage within to start your new venture now.

EVOLVE: Learn to go with the flow of life and become more you.

NURTURE: Discover why it's essential to nurture your talents and yourself as you go through the process of reinvention.

TRANSFORMATION: Commit to your reinvention and embrace the new you!

If you've already started on your reinvention journey, you may want to dip into the particular sections that are relevant to you at the time. However you read the book, I hope it will bring you clarity, focus and happiness. In each of the eight parts, you'll find the following:

Definition: Short definitions invite you to think about what the word actually means to you and how it will play a role in your reinvention.

My story: Throughout the book I've shared my story with you, as I want you to know that I have walked the walk. I've been through the reinvention process and both struggled and soared. And although I'm now a successful Life Coach helping people to reinvent themselves, I will always be a student too – learning, evolving and changing. Being able to see things from both sides of a situation allows me to bring a flexible approach as a coach.

Exercises: In each part of the programme there are exercises that will help you connect with your deepest desires and learn about yourself. I've explained meditation, affirmations and visualizations on pages 9–12. If you're not familiar with these techniques, I recommend that you read that section before you begin the programme.

The exercises in each chapter are designed to gradually build as a programme, helping you work toward your reinvention goal and take that first step of action. I hope you find them interesting, fun and inspiring! There are sections to fill in throughout the book as you do the exercises as well as a journal at the end of the book. This will become your reinvention journal and you can refer to it again and again as you achieve this particular goal, or the next time you want to reinvent a different part of your life. Alternatively, you may prefer to work on the exercises separately in a more private notebook or journal. Do whatever feels most comfortable to you.

Successful reinventions: Every day I come across people who tell me their inspirational stories and I wanted to share some of them here. I'm hoping that you will connect with one or all of them, see some of yourself in their stories and realize that if they can do it so can you. The more I interviewed people from different walks of life for this book, the more I was reminded that we really aren't all that different from each other and no matter how we were raised and whatever our financial situation, we go through very similar emotional challenges and journeys. I believe we are all here to learn and to find our way home to feeling whole and content within and we all have our different ways of doing it. Some do it willingly and some wait until a situation pushes them to do so.

Overcoming barriers: I've included answers to some of the common questions I get asked, which I hope you will find useful if you have similar concerns.

Remember this: key points to remember from this part of the programme.

Affirmations and quotes: Ever since I was a teenager, I have loved quotes and affirmations. I used to cut them out of magazines and hand them to friends to inspire them, and I would have various ones in my diary and on my desk that made me feel good to read. This is my wish for the ones I have created for you. I hope they make you smile and inspire you to be all that you are capable of being.

Reinvention tools

Throughout the programme, I use meditation, visualization and affirmations. Refer back to this section as much as you need to until you feel more practised in using these tools.

Meditation: Everyone can meditate and it really is one of the most effective self-help tools. Research is continually proving more of the amazing benefits of meditation, including that it helps to lower blood pressure, improve concentration and decrease stress and anxiety. I am passionate about teaching meditation and sharing my passion for it, both as a teacher and as a student, because I have felt the benefits in my own life and seen how it has helped to improve the lives of my clients. In this book I share some of my favourite guided meditations with you, some of which I have recorded especially for this programme and that you can listen to for free by going to www.zenme.tv/reinventme/.

A common question I get asked all the time by people starting out in meditation is 'How do I switch my thoughts off?' So let's just clarify something here – we can't switch our thoughts off, even with meditation. We have about 60,000–80,000 thoughts a day, so when it feels busy in our minds it's because it is! However, what we learn through meditation is that we can choose what we focus on and practise over and over again, bringing our focus back to one thing. That might be our breath, a mantra, an affirmation or even a colour. For example, while meditating you might think, 'I forgot to write that email today. Oh no they will think I'm rude...' and then the train of thought and worry sets in. So when that thought comes, acknowledge it, but then bring your focus straight back to your breath, breathing in and out. When the next thought comes, because it will, again bring your focus back to your breath and so it continues. You will slowly start to become the observer of your thoughts and adopt a non-judgemental approach, just allowing the thoughts to pass by like clouds in the sky.

This practice for the mind is very similar to working your muscles at the gym – the more you do it, the easier it will become. And the most wonderful thing is that the more you practise, the more you will be able to use this skill in everything you do, becoming more present in every moment and able to give each thing you do your full attention. Meditation will also help you to become less reactive in situations where a considered response is more helpful – it allows you time to assess. So as you meditate, invite thoughts and noises around you to come and go and know that they are a reminder for you to bring your focus and awareness back to your breath.

Visualize: I learnt to visualize as part of my sports training when I was 13 years old and this tool has followed me through life like a dear friend. Visualization is more of an active meditation in that you are intentionally imagining something. When thoughts come and go, you can still go back to your breath to bring your focus back to what you are visualizing. I truly believe that visualizing a goal, task or dream as successfully accomplished helps you to achieve it in reality. When you go within and get still in both meditation and visualization you allow for your breath and thoughts to slow down a little and for a certain amount of space to appear between each thought. In this space, clarity, inspiration, intuition, peace and calm can appear. You allow yourself to connect with your true self and to feel connected to your deepest desires.

Affirmations: An affirmation is basically a positive statement we repeat over and over again. We create these statements for ourselves so that they can become our reality. I love using positive affirmations in my life, which is why I have included them at the end of each chapter. Feel free to adapt them or write your own.

It's important when creating the affirmation to remember to make them in the first person ie. 'I', and present tense not future tense. For example, 'I am strong', not 'I'm going to be strong.' 'I am full of energy and focused.' Writing these positive statements on your phone, diary or a vision board, and repeating them in your mind or out loud to yourself in the mirror, can really help you to achieve your goals.

1.

RECOGNIZE

Definition: to accept or be aware of something.

So let's dive in! It's time for you and I to embark on this journey of reinvention, open your mind and ignite your curiosity. The starting point of any reinvention is to look at yourself and your life as it is now and recognize what needs to change. The exercises in this chapter are designed to do just that, helping you to discover what you need to learn from the situation you are in now or have been in the past, so you can move on and not end up in the same place again. As you look within and start becoming aware of how you perceive yourself, it will bring to light what you need to change to live a more contented and fulfilled life.

It's true that if we keep doing the same thing, we'll keep getting the same result. Sometimes life can feel like it's on repeat and to make major changes we need to acknowledge that a pattern we are stuck in is no longer working. It's important to understand how we created this pattern and then do something to change it. For example, do you find yourself always having the same conversations about being unhappy in your job, in your relationship or where you live? Or maybe those things are good in your life, but there are aspects of your personality you want to change – perhaps you'd like to be more confident and have more self-belief; or maybe you want to be a more patient and a less angry person. Your reinvention may simply be about becoming more comfortable in your own skin.

Recognizing where you are at is something you have to consciously stop and do. It's all too easy to fill your schedule with all sorts of distractions to stop yourself from facing up to things, but it's important to work out exactly what it is you are not wanting to see and perhaps what you are running from. You are the only person who knows truly how you feel and you are the only person that can do something about it, so as you do the exercises in this section, I urge you to be honest with yourself.

Admitting to yourself, on a conscious and logical level, that you are in fact stuck, frustrated and unhappy is the first step to changing your life. Recognizing what needs to change is perhaps the hardest part of this programme, but once you've tackled that, you can begin your very exciting reinvention journey!

MY STORY: **Recognize**

I'd been working on Strictly Come Dancing *for six years and increasingly felt a deep unease. I tried to ignore this feeling, but soon realized my soul wasn't happy. I didn't feel inner peace the way I knew was possible and I wasn't my happiest self at work. I was 'successful' and work was fun and interesting, but it didn't fulfil me within.*

I realized that blaming everything and everyone for my unhappiness wasn't going to solve my problems and that feeling sorry for myself, and the fact that I felt lost, would only cause more pain. Many self-help books later, I turned my situation on its head and asked what do I need to learn from this? What will make me wiser? How can I turn myself inside out? What can I change within to become happier

> '**I spent 20 years of my life and energy competing against others, but now I spend my energy being the best version of myself.**'

and more content? It felt good after all the frustration, emptiness and self-pity to turn it on its head and start focusing on how I could connect to my deepest desires and what really made me happy.

I believe that to some extent we attract into our lives what we focus on and wish for. I recognized that I had an urge to travel, change or move. I was curious to explore a career change, a job where I could help people to succeed and find contentment. This is when I recognized it was time to change and began to take action to reinvent my life.

EXERCISE 1: Who Am I?

So let's get started with this simple exercise to discover how you see yourself at this moment in time. Grab yourself a pen and introduce yourself by filling out the blanks below:

Hi, I'm ....   and I'm ....

Throughout my workshops and retreats, I have heard many answers to this 'Who Am I?' question, such as 'Hi, I'm xxx and I'm a mum' or 'Hi, I'm xxx and I'm feeling lost, bored, sad.' When you say what you wrote down out loud, detect the emotion attached to it. Try it now. Does your statement make you feel excited or does it give you a heavy feeling in your stomach? Does it make you feel proud? Does it make you feel sad? It's such an interesting question to ask yourself because it really helps you to recognize how you identify yourself. Once you've done the exercise, then ask yourself if you would like to change the way you answer that question in the future? And, if so, what needs to change in your life for you to do so?

For years I struggled when people introduced me as 'Camilla, the dancer'. I'd think that's not who I am; I didn't want to be defined by my job, but actually for a time I guess I was 'Camilla, the dancer' as I'd let that part of my life consume me. While I understand why people introduced me in this way, I would much rather they had said, 'This is Camilla' and then for people to get to know me as a person, rather than as 'the dancer'. Nowadays, if I were to answer the same question, I would write: 'I'm Camilla and I'm content' or sometimes 'I'm Camilla and I'm happy.'

EXERCISE 2: Identify

This exercise will help you tune in to your deepest desires and get to the core of what you would like to reinvent in your life. Ask yourself the following questions and write down your answers:

What would I like to reinvent in my life?

....

How is it going to make me feel once I have done it?

....

If money was not an issue, would my answer to the first question be the same or different? If different, how?

....

If I reinvent myself, what impact will it have on me?

....

How will it affect my loved ones?

....

What in life would truly make me happy?

....

Did writing down answers to these questions help you to confirm in your mind what you want to change and the sacrifices you are happy to make to do it?

I find it fascinating how people answer the question, 'If money was not an issue...?' I remember a lady at one of my seminars who, with the biggest smile on her face, said, 'My answer would be the same.' She was so happy to have recognized the area she wanted to reinvent. She realized that it was something that was possible with a little rearranging and sacrificing. No matter how much money she had, her goal was the same and she was determined to make it happen.

EXERCISE 3: Before and after

Doing this exercise will raise your awareness of where you are right now and where you would like to go. It will make it easier for you to look at yourself in a new way and make positive changes.

1. Take a piece of paper, draw a circle in the middle and write in the circle 'Me now'. Then draw out from the circle as many lines as you need and write on them exactly how you feel, such as 'uninspired', 'lost', 'stuck', 'not good enough', 'tired', 'bored', 'scared' and so on. Write down all the words that come to mind.

2. Look at the words and consider whether this is the first time you have felt like this. If there were other times in your life

you felt exactly the same, write them down on the paper too. As you look at what you have written down, you will probably realize that those emotions are not supporting you in moving toward reinventing yourself. Neither are those feelings defining who you truly are.

3. Now, hold that piece of paper in your hand and as you read the words again notice how you are feeling. Consider for a moment that you have a choice –

you can hold onto that way of seeing yourself or feeling, because really that is all it is, a belief you have created about yourself, or you can decide to let it go completely. If you are ready, then go ahead now and rip up the piece of paper. Now that you have let go of that old way of perceiving yourself, notice how much lighter you feel.

4. Now it's time for you to design a new way forward – a new way for you, where you support yourself, and feel confident and motivated to do the things you really want to do. Let's reframe this pattern and get started on recognizing what your reinvention could look, feel and sound like.

5. Take a new piece of paper and this time write in the middle, 'Me after my reinvention'. Then again draw lines from the circle and write how you would ideally like to feel once you have successfully reinvented yourself. Imagine it in as many details as you can. Use positive words only, such as 'inspired', 'motivated', 'excited', 'content', 'free', 'creative', 'proud', 'confident', 'self-belief'. This is your chance to design your ideal situation as if nothing stood in your way, not even fear.

Did doing this exercise put your goal at the forefront of your mind and make it clearer what you are working toward? Did you recognize a negative pattern of emotions and how they were created in the first place?

Here's how you might use this exercise to overcome a particular barrier: for example, if you believe you are not good enough to go for a job promotion, step back for a moment and look at the situation logically not emotionally. Write down, 'Can I do the job?' 'Yes.' Then ask yourself, 'So why do I still not feel good enough and lack self-belief?' Maybe when you were younger, you were led to believe that you didn't have what it takes and that situation created a pattern that you have repeated since. Remember that was then and not now.

As you recognize when these feelings were created, it will help you to let them go and choose a new way of acting, creating a new positive pattern in your life, a new way of being. Remember it's as easy to choose to believe in yourself as it is not to believe in yourself. So choose to believe and allow your confidence to grow within.

Successful reinventions: Jane, actress and author

I had what many would consider the perfect life – a lovely job travelling the world as aircrew, a beautiful apartment, a nice car, a designer (albeit fake designer!) wardrobe and exotic holidays. So why at the age of 34 did I give all that up to enter a profession that boasts a 94 per cent unemployment rate?

When a dear friend, a cancer survivor, ironically drowned in a windsurfing accident and I at the same time managed to contract a virus on a work trip, I was suddenly made aware of how fragile and precious life is and that we should never take it for granted. My friend's legacy to me was to seize the day and to have the courage to follow my destiny.

I was aware that I was about to enter a profession with a high unemployment rate, but I hung up my wings, put my flat on the market and swapped my car for a bicycle to pay for drama school. Some people thought me brave; others were convinced I was mad, but I could no longer repress the creative force within me and I recognized that it was time to acknowledge and nurture it.

My big vision when I started training to become an actress was to one day perform in London's West End. It took me 18 years and a lot of hard work, but I did it – and more than once. My journey has not been easy – there have been hurdles to overcome and doubts and frustration along the way, but I'm so glad I recognized the signs when I did and made the move to reinvent myself.

I have had to make huge sacrifices, but that is the path I chose. Upheaval and uncertainty have all been part of the process, but through positive thinking and meditation I learnt to let go of negativity and trusted the universe to guide me. I learnt to embrace a simpler way of life, to appreciate what I have and not yearn for the latest gadget or designer handbag. I discovered that wealth is far from just a financial thing; I feel rich in so many other ways. The inner peace and happiness, as well as the friendships and the experiences I have encountered along the way, are something no amount of money can buy.

'I once heard a motivational speaker say, "You can like your job, you don't have to love it." I immediately thought to myself but why do something I only like if I can do something I love!'

Overcoming barriers

I'm in my fifties. Am I not too old for reinvention?

Only if you believe so. The only difference between doing it and not doing it is the belief that you can. I have a wonderful book of poetry written by a lady who wrote books her whole life, but never believed she would become a poet. Yet in her nineties she started writing poetry and her book was published shortly after she passed away aged 107. When I hold her book and read the poems, it always reminds me that it's never too late until we say it is.

I recognize the fact that I need to challenge myself, but I don't have the confidence to go back to work after years of being a full-time mum. What if my job has changed so much that I can't do it anymore?

It is common to feel this way, but remember that many women have been in this position before you and succeeded in going back to work. Take a refresher course if you need to, or read everything you can get hold of online to bring you up to date. And, perhaps most importantly, don't be scared to ask for help. There have been many times in my life when I put off asking for help. When I finally asked and people were helpful, I thought to myself 'Why didn't I just ask earlier?' I think I used to see it as a weakness to ask for help, but now I see it as a strength.

Remember this ...

⋑ You may meet resistance from people who allow their fears to project onto you and make you doubt your decision.

⋑ You only have one person to answer to and that's you.

⋑ Follow your intuition – that gut feeling is there for a reason.

'I am ready to change and
I embrace the unknown.'

'I have courage to make changes
and I believe in myself.'

2.
E_{GO}

Definition: Your idea or opinion of yourself, especially your sense of your own importance and ability.

The ego – one of my favourite subjects. Oh the irony of that statement! What I mean is, I love being able to discuss how the mighty ego can rule our lives. Reinvention can be difficult if it's your ego calling all the shots, making you hold on to a certain way of acting and living that doesn't make you happy or fulfilled. I believe that to find your true self, and what will really make you happy, you have to face the ego and decide whether you are going to let it run your life. The exercises in this chapter are designed to help you do just that. Of course, your ego won't disappear, but getting a slightly large ego in check, and not constantly feeding it is, in my opinion, one of the best gifts you can give yourself and a massive step toward connecting with the true you.

Many of us are affected by our ego on a daily basis. For example, if when you hand in an assignment at work, your happiness is riding on getting praise from your boss you may want to have a serious word with your ego. Do you really need that feedback if you know in your heart you've done a good job? Now let me just clarify, essentially there is nothing wrong with liking a compliment; the *wrong* lies in it starting to define you. If you're reliant on praise and don't get it, you may feel disheartened and upset, even lost. That means the ego has won and you have handed over the control of how you feel. The ego needs constant feeding to survive; it needs approval, and it needs to feel superior. Here's another example: I'll love it if you find this book helpful and inspiring, and it will warm my heart to hear of your success stories and happiness after following the Reinvent Me programme, but ultimately I'm not reliant on that feedback. It's not going to change who I am and how I feel. I am writing this book because it makes me happy to help others. My ego *wants* to be told the book is amazing, but I don't *need* to hear this because I know deep within that I have tried my best and that I have written with the truest intention in my heart to share with you what has helped me.

Your ego will also affect your behaviour. You may behave in a certain way simply to feed your ego, at the expense of being true to yourself. If you have an inflated ego, you may set yourself apart from others and always compete and compare. You may often feel superior, which can affect how you connect with people and how they view you. Have you ever been in a situation, perhaps at work or in a relationship, where your ego really came out to play, and you acted so differently from who you actually are or wish to be or against what you believe in? So differently that you didn't even recognize yourself, all just to protect your ego and make sure it didn't get bruised? Often when people fall out, it's because of miscommunication and the ego getting in the way of the truth. When you're going through any conflict, it's worth checking who is in charge of your emotions – you or your ego?

I imagine the ego as cocky, self-righteous and stubborn. Taking on the ego can be a challenging battle and not always a pretty one, but it is one worth fighting. Discovering what your ego has had you do and believe until this moment can be overwhelming and you may be surprised at what you unravel when you do the exercises in this chapter. If your reinvention goal means, for example, starting at the bottom of the career ladder, downsizing your house or having less money, that ego of yours may make you feel not good enough. Giving up the things that feed your ego can make you feel vulnerable, but it can also be a wonderful, enlightening and freeing experience, enabling you to move forward in a new and exciting way.

Maybe your reinvention isn't on this big scale. Maybe, you just want a different attitude to life? For example, if you're someone who's always been very opinionated and first to comment (your ego loves that!), perhaps you want to become a better listener, and more open-minded and flexible in your behaviour. I realize that this may be difficult in the beginning, but little by little, as you raise your awareness, the benefit of listening will outweigh the need to be right. You will begin to realize that just because you don't force your opinion upon others, or others disagree with you, doesn't make you any less of a person.

I've met many people who claim that a big ego was the key to their success, but I think that's debatable. I would like you to consider if there is another way, one that makes you content and happy in your behaviour. When we believe in our own hype, believing that we are all separate, 'success' is often either short-lived or camouflaging deep unhappiness and insecurity – the 'success' is often to the detriment of our own long-term contentment.

One thing I know for sure is that building ourselves up again, and changing and improving, becomes a little easier when we let go of who we used to be, or who we think we should be, and accept who we are now in this moment – and when we embrace that we are all one.

Do you want to discover more about your relationship with your ego and how it's aiding your journey or blocking it? Go ahead and dive right into the exercises in this chapter.

MY STORY: Ego

As a successful dancer, I constantly compared myself to other women and to the couples I was competing with – how they looked, how they dressed and their progress. Being told I was a fantastic dancer and being complimented on my looks became a matter of course, and my ego loved it!

The success also afforded me a lifestyle I'd dreamed of in those early days, once I made it onto the professional circuit. However, the fame, success and attention never sat easily with me. My parents had taught me to be humble and to be grateful for even the small things in life. I came to realize that when the ego takes over and starts running our lives these qualities are challenged hugely. When we start getting used to a certain type of lifestyle our values and beliefs can get lost. I went on a huge journey of discovery before I became a Life Coach and 'turned myself inside out' using some of the exercises you'll find in this chapter. I was finally able to connect with the truest version of myself, and then one day I had a 'light bulb' moment when I realized that I was being held back by my ego's fears and limited beliefs. This was a very important turning point in my career.

When I left Strictly Come Dancing in 2008 after winning the show, I knew I was ready to embark on a new journey to retrain, study and invest in my future, and I was ready to give up the fame and fortune to fulfil my dream of opening my own Life Coaching business.

Then some years later, in 2013, I believe my ego was challenged. By the way, this happens often when we make major changes – we get tested to see if we really have changed and have an opportunity to act the old way or the new way. My challenge was moving from being in front of the camera and part of the 'talent' on Strictly Come Dancing to being behind the scenes choreographing and supporting the dancers and celebrities. Considering that in the past I had endorsed brands as a celebrity, headlined at theatres and been a guest on TV shows, many people thought this behind-the-scenes role was an odd choice. But the difference was I didn't care! I went with what felt fun and right to me – I was no longer bothered about feeding my ego by being in the limelight. Choreographing was a creative role and I got to use my Life Coaching skills to support the couples, so it was win-win. Two things happened while I was doing this job that proved to me that I had my ego under control. One day standing at the side of the dance floor one of the other dancers asked, 'Don't you just want to be out there?' To which I replied without any hesitation, 'No, I'm so happy stood here watching you all execute the choreography and so proud of you all.' It was an amazing moment. I felt like I was able to observe the situation for what it was – a job, not my life or who I was.

Then a few weeks later my ego got tested again: the show had one of its biggest nights broadcasting from Blackpool, one of the most famous ballrooms in the UK, a ballroom that had been part of my entire journey and where my dream of becoming a famous *dancer had begun. I was asked to join a routine in a non-starring role to help it go smoothly. After we had performed, someone said to me, 'I don't know how you did that, I could have never done that.' I just smiled to myself for in that moment I knew my ego was in a good place. I didn't feel any less of a person to jump in and help in a non-starring role. I just felt happy and proud of what everyone had produced that day. I knew for sure that if my ego had still been in charge the whole situation would have played out differently.*

Being able to put your ego into perspective allows you to start over or to take on different exciting projects no matter where on the ladder you are. If you are not afraid to roll up your sleeves, start again at the bottom of the ladder and get your hands dirty, the opportunities for reinvention are endless. Imagine if my ego had stopped me from going back to a show I adore and love? I wouldn't have had five months of wonderful memories and friendships. In some ways I preferred being on the sideline because the schedule was more manageable and I actually had time to enjoy my job.

Of course there were parts of being in the spotlight I enjoyed. I loved the photoshoots, our wedding being in Hello *magazine and some of the freebies and perks that came with a celebrity lifestyle. However it was always the experiences I could share with my friends or family that were the most fun. But, believe me, when I closed my eyes at night and went through my daily gratitude list, not once did jumping the queue at a famous nightclub or getting the 'best' table in the restaurant ever make it on there.*

I can honestly say that with or without the limelight, I am the same person. When I look back at my career it's not the winning moments that spring to mind first; it's the people I met, the experiences I shared, the actual journey of getting there, the inspiration and kindness from strangers I met along the way. Those are the memories that make me smile and that I hold dearly – those are real and not my ego.

'When you are content to
be simply yourself and don't
compare or compete,
everybody will respect you.'
Lao Tzu

EXERCISE 1: What is truly important to you?

This exercise helps you get to the truth of what you really want in life. Put your ego to one side, keep an open mind and go with the first answers that come to you. Make a list of everything that is important to you from 1–10, with 1 being the most important. For example, family, life balance, security, excitement, money, career, relationship, exercise, travel.

1 ....

2 ....

3 ....

4 ....

5 ....

6 ....

7 ....

8 ....

9 ....

10 ....

How does this list compare to what you have in your life now and how those things are prioritized? Are you surprised by what you've learnt? Use your answers to work out how you might approach your reinvention and re-prioritize. If, for example, feeling secure is important, but you want a career change, you may want to re-educate yourself while in your current job. If, on the other hand, excitement is up there at the top, I'd say just make the move and work out the details later!

EXERCISE 2: Ego-buster

With this exercise, find out what's driving your ego and whether those things are a good fit for the real you.

How big is your ego?

Rate the size of your ego on a scale of 1–10, with 10 being the biggest ....

What feeds your ego?
Write down five things that feed your ego. For example, in the past I would have written things such as success, having a flashy car, people telling me I was an amazing dancer, feeling superior to people.

1 ....

2 ....

3 ....

4 ....

5 ....

What are your true qualities?
Write down five words that describe the true you. Don't think about this for too long. Those instinctive words are more likely to be from your soul than your ego. Examples might be loving, curious, kind, caring, creative.

1 ....

2 ....

3 ....

4 ....

5 ....

What can you learn from your answers? Is there a mismatch between what feeds your ego and the true you? If so, consider where you may need to make changes to bring more of the true you to your reinvention and in every situation in your life.

EXERCISE 3: Does your ego define you?

Be as truthful as you can while doing this exercise.
We all have an ego! We are just establishing if you
are running your ego, or whether it is running you.

Answer the following questions 'yes' or 'no' and explain why:

Does my relationship, sport or job define me?

....

Do I validate myself from being praised?

....

**Do my work or hobbies just boost my ego or do they
make me happy deep within?**

....

Do I rely on other people's approval of me or my work?

....

Do I often act out of character?

....

*The more you answered 'yes', the more you're defined by your
ego. Are you surprised by how much your ego is ruling your
life? As you become more aware of how much your ego has
a hold of you and your decisions, you are able to consider what
you need to be mindful of and what you perhaps want to
change or work on through your reinvention.*

EXERCISE 4: Are you ready to set yourself free?

It's one thing to be aware of how your ego is affecting your life, another to do something about it. Answer the following questions, explaining your answer:

Am I willing to give up some things that feed my ego (for example, money, success, attention, compliments)?
....
Am I concerned about not knowing who I am without this relationship, habit or job?
....
Am I willing to be vulnerable?
....

It's okay if you're not ready to let go of these things. Carry on as you are knowing that the option to change is there when you feel ready. If you are ready, be prepared to feel vulnerable – you are, after all, stripping back to basics. If you allow a feeling of vulnerability, you will rebuild from a true place within. Sometimes we have to side step or step down to move forward in a new way. The exercises in this book will support you through vulnerable times and help you face the fear of change. I know what it feels like to swap the familiar for the unknown, but, believe me, we have an immense amount of inner strength to get through times of change when we decide to connect to it.

Successful reinventions: Alex, actor

As a child I loved being the centre of attention, so I guess that was the sign of a big ego. I felt I was better than everyone else, mainly because many things came easily to me – I was good academically, as well as in sports and music. If people said I couldn't do something, I wouldn't stop until I had proved them wrong – I carried that through into my adult life.

Looking back I think having an ego helped me, as I never doubted I would succeed as an actor. However, this unwavering self-belief bordered on being cocky and a lot of my behaviour came from a place of insecurity. I thought I had to act a certain way to fit into the acting world and I cared so much about what others thought of me.

Straight out of university and for over 10 years I was a working actor, going from job to job fairly seamlessly. However, during a long-standing contract I became aware that I wasn't actually the person I wanted to be and I wasn't happy. I started to look at myself more closely and with the help of a Life Coach I realized I didn't like what I found. I was arrogant, narrow-minded and argumentative – not flattering qualities. In fact, if I met my younger me now I would probably have slapped myself!

I wanted to change, be happier, more content and like myself more. At the time I associated all my negative qualities with the acting industry and felt that I had allowed the job to define me, so I started to pull away. Now, many years on, I realize that it wasn't the job that needed changing, it was me. I started thinking about changing my job, moving to a new area and creating a new life. Doing so wasn't easy because my ego still loved being boosted by being on TV daily and being well paid, but I needed to know who I was now, without the big ego and without the job. I wanted to find out if people would like the real me.

It took for me to walk away from the business altogether and explore other avenues to find happiness. I became more compassionate, more honest and more of my true self – and this is not my ego speaking, this is what my wife and my friends have told me! I remember how vulnerable I felt in the beginning once I had made major personal changes. Going to social events where people already knew me from before took courage and it felt like I was learning how to be me all of the time, not just some of the time.

I now work in a business that requires me to be confident, but I know that isn't the same as being dictated to by my ego. And, funnily enough, when I work in the acting industry now, I enjoy it much more – it's fun and I'm finally completely comfortable in my own skin in that environment. I don't spend time trying to prove myself to others and worry about what people think about me because I know who I am and that's good enough for me.

Overcoming barriers

If I deal with my big ego, will I lose the confidence and drive to run my company as successfully as I do now?

Being driven and confident is not the same as being ruled by a huge ego. For example, when the ego is in charge, you are less likely to consider your employees' feelings and ideas and more likely to rule with an 'I' rather than a 'we' attitude. Letting go of some of that ego won't mean you lose your drive and confidence, but it will open you up to possibilities and conversations you never even realized were available to you. And you may find you have a newfound energy from not having to keep up the image of having all the answers all of the time.

I find it difficult to back down from an argument even when I know I'm in the wrong. How can I deal with this?

The ego likes to be right all the time to feel superior and sees backing down or saying sorry as a weakness rather than a strength. By not backing down and diffusing the situation, you are simply fuelling the egos on both sides and causing more hurt and upset for you and the other person. You may save face to a certain extent, but you lose so much more. So think about what you'll gain and don't worry about who was right or wrong – you will enjoy the feeling of liberation surrendering brings.

Remember this ...

≫ If your ego is in control, you're probably neglecting your true self.

≫ A big ego can get in the way of teamwork.

≫ A big ego can be very unattractive to the people around you.

'I am always enough.'

3.

INNOVATION

Definition: something newly introduced, such as a new method or device.

So are you now ready to walk the walk as well as talk the talk?! You have an idea of how you would like to reinvent your life, but where do you start? Often goals and dreams remain in our head because of that nagging, negative inner voice (we all have one) that tells us they are unobtainable or we are not worthy of achieving them. In this part of the programme, you'll discover why it doesn't have to be that way and how to innovate ie. how to start turning those dreams and goals into reality.

I'm not going to pretend it's easy to innovate – it may seem overwhelming at times – and that's why all too often people give up on their goals. And even though many people believe that money and luck play a part in realizing our dreams, what's more important are, in fact, perseverance, commitment, discipline and willpower.

I have had many ideas throughout my life and set myself many goals that seemed unobtainable at first. But by breaking those goals down into achievable parts, keeping the vision and working hard, I have turned them into reality. I've realized over time that the more I commit to making my goals and ideas a reality, the more I achieve them. I have built up inner confidence and belief that having done it once, I can do it again.

You may feel that your ideas or dreams are out of reach, too complicated and too big. It's common to feel this way in the beginning. So many people have told me they were overwhelmed when they first started out on their quest and that they had no idea how to make what they really wanted happen.

To achieve a goal you need to break it down into manageable chunks and then tackle it step by step. As they say, 'Rome wasn't built in a day' – maybe not in a day, but let's remember it still got built eventually! Take, for example, a middle-aged man whose dream it is to become a long-distance runner and one day complete a marathon. If he had the idea one day and then tried to run the marathon the following week or month, he'd be highly likely to fail. Instead, he starts with small goals and gradually builds up the stamina and skills he needs to successfully run a marathon one day. He follows a very specific plan – perhaps starting with a 5k race, building up to a 10k race and then a half marathon. Maybe he also takes some practical measures such as eating a healthy diet that supports his running, giving up smoking and seeking the advice of other long-distance runners on how to train. If you break down your ideas into smaller goals in much the same way, the whole thing becomes much less overwhelming and more achievable.

It can help to read about or talk to others who have realized their dreams – those who have overcome fears and adversity and made small ideas into big successes, whether personally or in business. I remember someone telling me years ago, if you want to do something surround yourself with people who have already done it or others who you feel inspired by.

So how do you handle that negative voice? We are brilliant at talking ourselves out of a good idea with thoughts like, 'It's been done before', 'I don't have the resources to follow this through', and 'I don't know how to make this happen'. But, believe me, you are undoubtedly far more resourceful than you give yourself credit for! Those negative thoughts are normal, but just remember that every time a thought like that comes into your mind you have a choice – you can believe that thought or you can make a conscious decision to switch it and think the exact opposite. For example, 'I don't know how to make this happen' becomes 'I will make this happen' or 'It's been done before' becomes 'Similar things have been done before, but I'm putting my spin on it and my passion into it, which will make it unique.'

When people ask me, 'What can I do to make this happen?' I say, 'You can begin by getting started,' so what are you waiting for? Take a look at the exercises in this chapter and let's innovate!

MY STORY: **Innovation**

I have had to innovate many times in my life, not least by moving to England to fulfil my dream of becoming a champion dancer and then to California to fulfil my dream of becoming a Life Coach. Many people tell me I'm lucky and assume it was easy for me, but none of it came about by me choosing a point on a map and then wishing myself there. It came about by having an idea, making a plan and working out the steps I needed to take to achieve my goal.

When I first dreamt of moving to California in my thirties, that was all it was – a dream. I wanted to innovate both my professional and personal life. I wanted a better balance and to live an outdoor lifestyle in a place where I wasn't defined by being a successful professional dancer and celebrity. After a few years I started researching what it would take to make this a reality. I asked people who had made such a move what it entailed. There were people who were helpful and people who weren't, and there was advice that put me off and advice that encouraged me.

In the end I considered all the information I had gathered, followed the advice that felt right in my gut and sat down and wrote a plan of what I needed to do. This included moving out of our house and renting it out, putting our belongings in storage and living with family for a while to save money. It involved applying for a working visa, finding somewhere to live and planning what to do once we got there. And so it went on, until 18 months later when we found ourselves actually living in California!

Once we had moved, I had to keep being mindful of the fact that I wanted to find balance in my life, given that it had been top heavy with work for most of my life. This meant not allowing work to take over my life again like it had in the past and allowing myself to have time off to do the things I enjoy, such as having more time with my husband, walking the dogs, spending time outdoors and studying new things. It also meant making mindful decisions when it came to our lifestyle, such as the size of the property and car we chose. I had learnt that everything in life has its price, taking up our time and energy often to the detriment of time for ourselves, and our families and friends.

'A journey of a thousand miles must begin with a single step.'
Lao Tzu

Another dream I turned into reality was to write my first book, Strictly Inspirational. *I didn't, however, have that idea and turn it into reality overnight. I wrote down ideas and thoughts that I then turned into a book proposal. I spoke to people about how to get a book published. I found the right publisher. It all took time, work and rejections before it eventually happened. It's been the same with this book – it started with an idea for a self-help programme. I then worked the idea up slowly, interviewed people and worked with the publisher, then I started writing it, chapter by chapter.*

Sometimes it's just good to start, even if you're not sure where your idea will go. Often when I sit down to brainstorm a new magazine article, I have an initial idea but it's not until I actually start writing that the full picture emerges. There has to be an element of trusting the process. I tend to 'jump', ie. I commit, and then I work out how to 'swim', ie. then work out the finer details.

When I choreographed dance routines, it was a similar process. I knew the end result I wanted, so I would work backwards: how many dancers do I need? What sort of story do I want to tell with my choreography? I would always start by writing down the things I was sure of and then add the other parts as I went along. I also learnt a long time ago that making mistakes along the way is okay as long as we learn from them. Some of the best dance steps I ever created with my partner came from going wrong – in that moment it was as if magic happened and something unique was created. I remember fondly people asking about a specific step we did and knowing that it happened by 'mistake'! So to innovate there has to be a certain amount of planning but also a certain amount of evolving – something we'll look at later in part 6.

EXERCISE 1: Making a plan

Let's get to work and take that first step together by making a plan.

Ask yourself:
What can I do today to start my reinvention plan?

....

Think of one thing, however small, that will bring you a step closer to your goal. Write it down.

....

Then carry on with the list...
What's the second thing I can do in a week's time?

....

Then...
What can I do in a month's time?

....

Do you have an entire plan? Don't worry if there are gaps to fill out later. It's important to leave room to be flexible and modify things as you go. Once you have these steps written down it will help you to feel more focused and clear about your journey and make it easier to get started.

EXERCISE 2: Meditation – 'Planting the seeds in the garden of opportunity'

This meditation is a great way to kick-start your reinvention. It is one of my favourite meditations and I hope you are going to love it as much as I do. I created it because meditation is such a big part of my life and I have experienced such amazing benefits. I will go as far as to say meditation has changed my life. Before you begin, if you're new to meditation, you might want to read the general guidance on pages 9–11.

When we get still and allow ourselves time in silence we allow ourselves to connect with our intuition, inspiration and calmness within and this has a very powerful effect on our minds. We allow the anxiety to settle and the voice of doubt to subside and instead invite in clarity and focus.

So are you ready to plant your seed, ie. your idea, goal and dream, in the garden of opportunity and wait for the innovation to happen? If so, let's go!

Sit or lie down somewhere comfortable, where you will not be disturbed. Close your eyes or lower your gaze. Sit rather than lie down if you think you may fall asleep. Bring your awareness to your breath. Notice where in your body you feel your breath and then just allow it to be exactly there.

We have about 60,000–80,000 thoughts a day, so thoughts will come and go throughout the meditation. Instead of resisting them, just allow them to come and go and each time you notice a thought let it be a reminder to bring your focus back to your breath.

Start counting as you breathe in 1, out 2, in 3, out 4 and so on until you reach 20. Repeat this a few times until you start to feel relaxed. Then imagine that you are walking into the most beautiful garden you have ever seen. Notice all the trees and the flowers and any other surroundings. This is your garden of opportunity.

As you look around the garden and all its beauty, you start to realize it's all created simply by the seeds that were planted and then nurtured. Consider for a moment that when we plant a seed in the garden, we don't stand over it and say, 'Grow, grow, hurry up.' No, we plant it and walk away knowing that it will grow with water, sun and air.

Imagine now if your ideas, dreams and goals can do the same. See yourself holding a seed in your hand that represents your idea or dream. Now plant it somewhere in the garden.

After you have planted it, sit for a minute and imagine this seed growing and blooming and turning into an amazing flower or tree, just like your idea or dream blossoming and happening.

Imagine yourself taking steps of action toward making it happen. Notice what it feels like, sounds like and looks like as you imagine doing some of these things.

Finally, imagine what it will feel like once you have achieved it and your innovation has happened. How do you feel? Are you happy, excited, calm? Just notice what you notice without judgement and then go ahead and open your eyes knowing that you have successfully planted your seed in the garden of opportunity.

How did you feel after the meditation? You might want to write down your thoughts and feelings. Repeat this exercise as often as you like and plant as many seeds as you wish in your garden of opportunity. To listen to this free guided meditation, go to http://www.zenme.tv/reinventme/.

Successful reinventions: Tine, youth counsellor

I guess I've always been an innovative person. When I finished my degree in English Literature, aged 24, I immediately wanted to go in a completely different direction. I had always considered myself a creative person and I wanted to explore that side of myself in more depth. So, I decided to take a degree in design and textiles before I went on to set up a successful shop selling my own designs. I had succeeded in proving to myself, rather than others, that I was capable of achieving whatever I set out to do, but I found that gradually my ego started to grow. I got used to people telling me they loved my designs and how clever I was, which I enjoyed at the time. However, a few years in, I started to realize that although I felt extremely lucky to be running a successful business, it had begun to feel superficial. I noticed that I felt alone and pretty empty inside and I didn't want to feel this way any longer. I knew things had to change and so began the next step of my reinvention ... I decided to study psychotherapy.

Innovation is all about taking steps toward your goal and each time I had a new idea to pursue, I didn't immediately know how it would work out, but I started with something I could do: for example, with design I took a course and learnt about textiles etc. With psychotherapy, I found the right education, studied and built up my own practice and kept adding to this by taking a degree in teaching and personality psychology. This path led me to becoming a youth counsellor, a role that I love and that gives me so much fulfilment. Although this was a complete career change, I still use my creativity to connect with and help people when counselling.

I have learnt so much about myself through my reinvention journey. I'm now in my late forties and my priorities are certainty and security, which weren't as important to me when I was younger. Even so, I will never sacrifice my own happiness for a job that is no longer in line with my values and beliefs, and if that means walking away and starting over again I will do it in a heartbeat. I will keep living, evolving and inspiring in the way that is true to me.

Everything I have learnt has brought me to where I am today. Innovation for me has been key in life, both personally and professionally, as I'm a curious human being with a need to constantly evolve and change. No matter how small or big the change or goal has been and no matter the challenges, I have always had a strong, yet almost naïve, inner belief that somehow it will all work out.

Overcoming barriers

I'm scared of failing. How can I get past this fear to take that first step?

Two things really help to get past the fear: firstly, focus on what you are good at, the skills that you know you have – this will boost your confidence immediately because whatever the innovation, there will be one part that you know you can totally nail. Secondly, research as much as you can; draw knowledge and inspiration from people who have successfully done something similar and learn from their mistakes. Look for relevant online courses too.

In the past I went ahead with ideas that failed and ended up out of pocket at times, because I didn't do enough research – that's how I learnt and now I know better. However, I don't see those attempts as failing because they have provided me with the foundation for what I do today and taught me valuable lessons such as researching, being patient and, above all, believing in myself. For me, the biggest failure would be not trying and then having regrets.

I'm usually a very impatient person, so the idea of breaking my goal down into small steps is not appealing. How can I get over wanting everything right now?

I can totally relate to this. Learning to have patience and trusting in the process of change was a major challenge for me, but one that has helped me tremendously in my life. Although I often wanted everything right now, I learnt that breaking down a goal doesn't mean you will get there any slower – quite the opposite, in fact. By breaking it down you allow yourself to be fully focused on what needs to be done in the moment, rather than wasting valuable time speculating on what needs to be done tomorrow or a week from now; this makes you efficient and gives you clarity to focus fully. Also as part of this slower and steady journey, you're likely to learn valuable lessons and skills along the way, which will put you in a better and stronger position once your goal does come to fruition.

'An idea born out of passion will have enough fire in its belly to make it a reality.'

Remember this ...

∋ Many of the most brilliant, genius ideas were once dismissed or laughed at, but later applauded.

∋ Focus on the 'When I achieve it' instead of asking yourself 'How is it going to be possible?'

∋ Don't be put off by the fact that others have similar ideas – yours will have its own unique twist, plus the passion you will bring to it.

'I commit to taking action
and trust all will become clear
as I keep moving forward
step by step.'

'I trust in my own ability and
take action toward my goals
every day.'

N^{4.}ow

Definition: At the present time or moment.

So by now you have made a plan and planted your seed. Well done, that is awesome! But to make that plan happen, to nourish that seed, you need to take action. And what better time to do that than NOW!

NOW is such an important concept and word – and so vital to reinventing yourself – not only because you need to make changes NOW rather than putting them off for a while, but because NOW will also remind you to be present *in the moment*. When you are not dwelling on the past or worrying about the future, when you are mindful of the present, you will listen to your intuition, make better decisions, become less fearful of what might happen and really live through and learn from your journey of change.

Like so many people you may be '*thinking* of making changes'. When I hear this, I often wonder when that will change from 'I'm *thinking* of' to 'I'm *going* to'. The fascinating process we go through before we commit to change goes like this: I'm thinking of it, I'm ready, I'm going to do it, I'm doing it now and then, of course, I've done it! That's not to say that an idea can't marinate before it flourishes, but we must give it the attention it needs to develop. It may not happen right this moment, but at least you are taking the appropriate action toward your goal.

If I had to take a guess at what was holding you back from turning your innovative plan into action, I'd guess that it's fear. Am I right? So many people become paralyzed by fear: fear of failing, fear of not being good enough, not clever enough, fear of not having enough money. This is very common – it's part and parcel of being human. But let me ask you this: what about the fear of not living your life to its fullest potential? Why are you not fearful of that? Surely we are all obliged to do the best we can with the precious life we have been given? The exercises in this chapter will help you address and get into perspective those fears that may be holding you back.

Another way people avoid the now is by telling themselves, 'I haven't got time. I'll deal with it later'. The problem is things get put off again and again and then you end up resenting that you didn't take action when you had the opportunity. Being 'too busy' can easily become an excuse for not doing it NOW, so schedule in time to work on your reinvention.

Choose something from your plan, nourish that seed – it won't grow unless you feed it. You'll feel so much better when you take action than when you avoid it. It's just like when you put off a phone call because it's going to be a little uncomfortable. Then once you make the call you find it isn't that bad; afterward you feel relieved and wonder why you'd put it off for so long. Sound familiar?!

Sometimes it takes major events like a relationship break-up or other types of loss, illnesses or accidents for us to wake up and make changes. But it doesn't have to be this way. Change can be much more positive and proactive: don't wait for life to happen, instead choose to make time for whatever changes you want to make and all the goals you would like to achieve. Listen to that all-important intuition and you will know when the time is right for you.

'Taking steps of action is like planting lots of seeds. Eventually you will have a beautiful garden.'

When you are making changes, whether professionally or personally, it's so important to stay in the now. If you think about many years ahead – for example, try to map out in your head a complete career change or the next five years – it can be stressful and overwhelming. You're quite likely to give up there and then. If you stay in the now – and think about what you can control in *this* moment, rather than worrying about those things you can't predict – you can allow yourself to take it one step at a time and really tune in to your intuition. Through tools such as meditation and other mindfulness techniques that you will learn throughout this programme, you can learn to live in the moment.

For a while I have been wearing a watch that says 'NOW' instead of showing the time. So when I look at it, I am always reminded to be present in the moment – this has really helped me. I used to feel quite challenged by the idea that we only had now, until I accepted that the past has gone and the future is still to unfold so we had better just make the most of this moment!

By being mindful – by living more in the now – you will also live a fuller, richer life. You will live the experience of making changes, both the good parts and the bad, and you will come out stronger on the other side. Looking back, I realize that I ran through my life, especially through my twenties, far too quickly. I was so fearful of not achieving my goals, and so busy thinking about a future goal, that I completely forgot to be present, to enjoy my journey. One day one of my dancing coaches reminded me to start enjoying each moment and to treasure all the little goals along the way to the big one because the victory is short-lived, and then all you have are the memories of the journey. This advice totally changed my outlook and it's something that has stayed with me ever since.

I have clients who come to me so stressed. When we start to talk and I get to the bottom of their concerns, I often find they are worrying about the future, about what will happen five years from now when their children have left home, when their partner has retired or if their relationship doesn't work out. These are all things they can't possibly know about or predict, yet they ruin so much of the now by worrying about those things. They forget to enjoy the present moment with their partner or the kids who are living with them now and instead worry about what it would feel like when they are gone. Learning to live in the now can help us in so many ways in life – as we become more present, we start to trust the process of life and we are less anxious because we are not worrying about things that may or may not happen in the future. Instead we enjoy the being, the planning and the learning in the now.

Even now, I can be at a social event and find myself thinking about a workshop I need to prepare for later in the week. Before I know it, I'm worrying and planning and missing valuable time with family and friends. I have to remind myself to let it go and bring myself back to the moment. Do you ever go to a party or a family gathering and spend time on your phone wishing you were somewhere else or worrying about the work you have to do? Well, this is a classic situation of not being in the now. Like all the techniques I'm going to share with you in this book, being mindful – being present to the here and now – is something you have to constantly work on, but I hope, like I have, you find that it enhances your life.

MY STORY: Now

Each time I've made big life changes I've felt fearful, but I decided a long time ago that greater than any of these fears would be to die without having tried in every way I could to reinvent myself personally and professionally. Dying without having tried became my motivation to get on and do it now rather than waiting for the perfect moment.

To overcome fear of the unknown, it helps to have an emergency plan in place. When I left Denmark for the UK, I told myself I could go back to my job as an estate agent if it didn't work out. When I moved to California to be a Life Coach, I told myself I could always go back to dancing. My mum always told me not to burn bridges, so I kept that in mind and it has been a very helpful tool. I found that once I had addressed my fear and made an emergency plan, I could move forward knowing that I would never want to use the emergency plan but that it was there – in the same way we know where the emergency exit is on a plane, but we hope we will never need to use it.

Now is all about making the most of opportunities. Once I knew I wanted to be a motivational speaker, I'd listen to other speakers, such as Marianne Williamson, Oprah Winfrey and Anthony Robbins, and imagine one day what it would feel like to be up there, like them, in front of an audience. Then one day a friend rang me up out of the blue and asked if I fancied doing a motivational speech for her staff. The thought of speaking in front of an audience for 30–45 minutes scared me a lot, but I still said yes. I thought now is as good a time as any to get started and I will work out how to structure my talk once I have committed. It would have been so easy to turn down this opportunity and say I wasn't ready. I could have waited for the 'perfect time', but when would that have been? I started structuring my speech by starting with something I knew – I jotted down a few motivational tips I was certain had helped me in my career and that I knew would be helpful to people. I wasn't Anthony Robbins yet but it was personal to me, and this is one thing I realized back then – always put your personal twist on it. When we are truly authentic it shines through – so rather than trying to be someone else, always use your uniqueness. I got the audience up on their feet to dance for a few seconds because that made me feel at ease and broke the ice.

The first time I led a group meditation I felt nervous to the point of thinking, 'I can't do this'. I had done meditations for years, but only with one client at the time. It took a couple of classes before I completely relaxed and allowed myself to enjoy it, and I quickly felt as if I had come home. It's now one of my favourite things in the world. I'm so happy that I faced the fear and took the opportunity when it came my way; I knew it was time.

When I was so focused on my goals and not present in the moment, my judgement would be clouded on certain things and instead of having clarity I'd feel confused, fearful and stressed. I would go over a situation again and again in my head. I would let a rude email ruin my mood or, even worse, reply before having thought it through. These days it's not that I don't get annoyed or have a day of feeling off, but I have tools up my sleeve, tools like the ones throughout this book, that bring me back to where I'm happy to be. It's a bit like walking down the middle of a road – sometimes the wind blows us off to the side or people pull us off, but with practice and mindful tools we know how to get ourselves back to the middle again.

EXERCISE 1: Now is the time

This exercise is designed to help you face some of your fears so that they no longer become barriers standing in your way of change.

Write down the worst thing that could happen if your reinvention plan doesn't work out?

....

Now you've written down your worst fear, does it seem irrational? Perhaps it's not as bad as you imagined. By facing up to the worst that can happen, we know exactly what's at stake and realize that this scenario may not be so far off the situation we are already in. Because often by the time we take action, we have hit rock-bottom emotionally and we know something has to change. If you have children, you will, of course, have to consider how the changes will affect your family as a whole. Most of us have friends who would put a roof over our heads or help us out in other ways at challenging times. Consider what you will do if things don't work out.

2. Write down your emergency back-up plan

....

3. Write down the pros and cons of making changes now. Use a separate piece of paper to write them in two columns.

4. When you are considering whether now is a good time to start, ask yourself these questions:

What would happen if I succeed at my reinvention?

....

What would happen if I don't succeed at my reinvention?

....

What would happen if I start taking action today?

....

What would happen if I don't take action now?

···

What wouldn't happen if I take action now?

···

Be guided by your answers. Having answered the questions, does making changes seem less of a big step? Can you now see a way of changing your situation? Let's say you are bored and stuck in your life, seeking adventure. If you stay in the situation exactly how it is now without changing anything, nothing is going to change is it? Changing a few things could help you become unstuck.

The other day a friend told me she has decided to move to Australia. She is not going for eight months, but by making the decision something has shifted within her. She feels excited about planning the move – it's like a light has been switched on within her. Whether she goes or not, she has started opening up to new possibilities – making a plan, taking action toward something that excites her. This in itself will start to attract different things into her life. She is already being introduced to people who know people in Australia. Who knows where it will lead eventually but she has done something to make a change.

EXERCISE 2: Fear-buster map

Let's get to it and bust that fear box right open!

Take a piece of paper and pencil. Ask yourself:
1. What are my fears?

2. What are my doubts?

Write them down.

Doubts can be feelings such as frustration, lack of confidence, low self-esteem. Take a good look at the paper. Are those fears and doubts facts or just your perception of yourself or someone else's opinion of you? When were they created? Has something happened earlier in your life to create them? Could you consider that these are not facts and this is not happening now? Once you're aware of fears and doubts, you can let go of them and instead create a new way of looking at your reinvention without the doubts and fears.

Do you want to let got of those fears and doubts?
Rip up the paper and let's reframe it:

Take a new piece of paper and write down
My ideal situation for achieving my goal

Write words and sentences like: I'm confident, I feel supported, I believe in myself, I know I can do it, I'm excited, happy, fun, patience, proud of myself.

Now how do you feel? Writing down your thoughts and feelings will help you here.

EXERCISE 3: Letting go

Try this quick yet powerful exercise to help you let go of your doubts and fears:

1. Sit somewhere where you can fully relax.

2. Close your eyes and imagine you are holding onto a string that is attached to a rather large balloon – make it any colour you like!

3. Now imagine sticking all of your fears and doubts onto that balloon. How does that look and feel to you? Imagine all of those words now attached to the balloon. Take a deep breath and then as you next exhale, let go of the string and let go of those emotions. Allow the balloon to float far, far away up into the sky – until it's so tiny that you can no longer see it and then suddenly it's completely gone.

4. As you take another breath, you know you have let it go and that you can open your eyes and notice a newfound clarity and focus.

How do you feel? Has a weight of worry been lifted from your shoulders? Write down your thoughts and feelings if you wish.

EXERCISE 4: Be present meditation

To learn to be present in the moment and connect with your intuition, try this short 3–5 minute meditation. Tie in the words below to the rhythm of your breath. It works like a positive affirmation meditation.

Breathe in: 'I'
Breathe out: 'Am'
Breathe in: 'Here'
Breathe out: 'Now'

Repeat this for a few minutes and then switch with the words 'I am connected to my intuition', again just using one word per breath in and one per breath out.

By doing this daily, you will start to notice when you are not present and a quick breath with the words 'I am here now' can bring you back to the present.

Successful reinventions: Emma, jewellery designer

I gave up running my thriving PR company, and the wealth and success that came with it, to become a jewellery designer, but my reinvention was about much more than a career change. Looking back I realize I had started my reinvention on a personal level a while before I started it professionally. I had been attending Reiki and self-help weekend courses for some years and meditation had become a constant in my life. One day I suddenly woke up to the feeling of let's get my life and work in harmony. Let's take back the control of my life NOW.

I'd been aware of the voice within me getting louder and louder and it got more and more difficult to ignore. However, for quite some time I didn't listen – I wasn't present! My intuition was trying to tell me I was feeling disconnected in life and that my job was not fulfilling me on a creative or personal level – in fact, it felt soul-destroying. I guess a turning point was when I mentioned to my parents that I thought it would be cool to do something completely different, such as become a yoga instructor or an art teacher, or even explore acting which I'd always wanted to do. They felt I would be wasting my university degree and that I'd be crazy to walk away from all I'd achieved, but I thought, 'Yes, but I'd be happy!' That's when I started thinking about taking designing more seriously and the idea to become a jewellery designer was planted. My goal was to design pieces that were mindful and that would have a deep meaning for me and for the person wearing them.

Somehow, with perseverance and the belief that this was also my personal journey, it slowly came together. I started to feel more connected and in tune with myself and my jewellery company was born, but by no means flying just yet. There was a long road ahead, and if I had really known what it would take to succeed I probably wouldn't have started it. Holding the finished product in my hand was a very special moment, but it did not happen lightly. I had to make huge sacrifices, including moving in with my parents and couch-surfing with friends for two years. At times this felt extremely frustrating and I would have moments of huge self-pity and thoughts like 'I used to have this and now I don't.' I'd feel envious and worried, and wonder if I had made the right decision.

There was something unsettling about not having my own base, but it taught me a lot. When you are physically no longer in a place of security, your home where you feel safe, you have to go within yourself to find that safe and calm place. Meditation throughout all of this has been my guidance, my calm and my rock.

Overcoming barriers

I worry about the future all the time. What can I do to overcome this anxiety?

Writing down exactly what is worrying you will help you rationalize it and calm your confused and stressed feelings. Look at the things you have written down and decide one by one, on a logical level, if you can take action to solve any of these concerns now. Then find a few minutes to do the 'Be present' meditation on pages 82–3 and the Letting Go exercise on pages 81–2. Once you have finished, you will find you are less likely to worry about the things in the future that you can't deal with now and instead focus on what you can change in this present moment.

I'm unhappy in my relationship, but I'm scared of leaving because I don't want to be alone. What should I do?

Many people have to face feeling alone at some point in their lives. It was a huge fear for me too when I left a long-term relationship, but then I accepted that we are always alone in some sense, we just have different people walking along the path with us through life. When we get comfortable about being alone, we start making different decisions – our decisions aren't made from a place of fear, but from a place of abundance, where we can create and get excited about all the possibilities in our lives. I hope the exercises in this book will help you overcome your fears and help you reach a decision that is right for you.

Remember this ...

⋙ We have an intuition for a reason. I chose a long time ago to allow it to guide me. When we really listen to our intuition, it will guide us toward noticing when it's time to make changes.

⋙ The most amazing present you can give yourself is to become present in every moment; it makes each experience much more special. This truly is the key to living mindfully.

⋙ You create your own luck by taking action toward your goals.

'I reach my goal because I am committed. I take action every day, step by step, task by task. I am doing it!'

'I make things happen by taking action every day and I'm proud of myself.'

5.

VISUALIZE

Definition: to form a mental image of something incapable of being viewed or not at that moment visible.

In a sense we are jumping from 'Now' to the future because this chapter is all about visualizing your reinvention – imagining that reinvented you! I also like to think of V as standing for 'Venture'. Put the two Vs together and they make a perfect team – by the end of this chapter you will be visualizing your daring new venture!

Visualizing is such a powerful tool and one I use a lot. I truly believe that if you can visualize yourself after your reinvention it will help to bring the goal closer to you. When we can see something clearly in our minds, it helps it to become more tangible, which motivates us to keep believing we can achieve it. For example, if you are looking to reinvent your relationship, you might have an image of how it would look and feel to improve things with your partner. If spending more quality time with each other is part of your reinvention, maybe you could visualize a wonderful vacation together or a situation at home where you are enjoying cooking together. Simply picturing these positive scenarios will help you feel better about your relationship.

If you are single and feel ready to settle down, you might want to visualize your ideal partner. Sounds crazy, eh?! Well I did it, and am now happily married to the guy! When someone suggested that I write down the qualities I was looking for in my ideal man and then visualize having that person in my life, I was like 'Yeah, right, as if that's going to work!' Well, how wrong I was. It was like by doing so I made an agreement with myself and with the universe that I would focus on what I really wanted. It wasn't until a few months into the relationship that I thought to myself, 'OMG, he actually has all the qualities I wrote down and visualized' – that was a pretty cool moment. Since then I have held many workshops sharing these tools and they totally work.

If your reinvention is about losing weight or becoming fitter, you might picture yourself eating healthy food and exercising. You could visualize how you look and feel once you have achieved your goal, perhaps imagining yourself feeling happy and confident about your body, and eating a healthy meal at a favourite restaurant. Many famous athletes swear by visualization to improve their game and skills – they may be physically fit, but be held back mentally because they don't see themselves as winners. Visualizing achieving their goals gives them self-belief and the mental strength to succeed. I used visualization successfully throughout my dancing career, and I have used this awesome tool with so many different clients to help them overcome nerves in all sort of situations, from public speaking to taking part in competitions.

Visualizing is something that comes quite naturally to us as children, but then somehow, as we grow up, we forget how to do it, or we write it off as a waste of time. As a child you may have imagined future things, such as what it would feel like to ride a bike, to get married or to drive a car. This kind of daydreaming is not that different from purposely imagining how we would like a change or goal to turn out, but as adults we stop ourselves having this kind of childish fun. We simply don't dare to dream. We stand in the way of our own creativity and intuition, thinking that our goal is silly. But why? What if visualizing something helps make it happen? Have you thought about that? How cool would that be?!

Remember that visualizing is free and a playful experience – don't get caught up in the how to, such as not having the money to achieve some of your dreams, but rather allow your imagination to flow freely. I have heard so many amazing stories of people who have achieved their dreams and goals against all the odds. A friend of mine would regularly walk around the area where he wanted to live, but couldn't afford. He would visualize what it would be like and feel like to drive up and park at a particular house that he loved and for that to be his home – and after some time, it became a reality! I used to walk past a fancy couture shop in Knightsbridge, London, dreaming about one day wearing one of those very expensive dresses. I knew it was not going to happen with my hourly pay of £6.50, but it didn't stop me from visualizing what it would feel like and look like – and I did many years later wear many dresses from that shop!

I think there is a reason why we have been given such a powerful tool – we can use our imagination to go anywhere in the world, to picture any situation just by thinking of a memory, a new situation or a goal. I'm so excited about you trying the exercises in this chapter and allowing yourself to connect with that child-like, creative part of you. Let your imagination take you anywhere you want to go as you visualize the future you!

MY STORY: Visualization

My first experience of visualization was when I was 13 years old. I remember it so clearly. I was struggling to perfect a step in a dance routine and the more frustrated I got, the more I couldn't do it. My dance coach asked me to stop what I was doing and take a break. He told me to sit down, close my eyes and become aware of my breath, and then when I felt relaxed to start imagining myself doing the step correctly. I found it really challenging; at first it was so much easier to visualize it going wrong than right. But each time I closed my eyes and imagined a step, it became slightly easier.

As my dancing career progressed, I visualized other things, such as what it would look, sound and feel like to win a specific competition. Later on I visualized living in another country and, just like that, active visualization became a part of my life. I used to dream about living in California. I would walk along the seafront in Denmark and visualize the difference in temperature between Denmark and California, imagining the trees, flowers and smells there. It was surreal when I finally moved to Los Angeles and took my first trip to the beach; it felt like I had walked there before. I had visualized it in my mind for so long that I felt completely at home when I got there.

Another great visualization tool I've used to support my dreams and goals, and that you can learn in this chapter, is a vision board (see Exercise 2 on pages 100–101). Make a board of pictures and thoughts and feelings that exactly describe and show how you would like your life to look after your reinvention. I have literally put everything on my vision boards I wanted to achieve, from meeting my ideal partner to buying my first house to connecting to my Zen within and, of course, for manifesting my dream jobs

One thing I've learnt when using vision boards is that you have to be specific. I remember doing a fabulous vision board in 2007, one that made me feel full of joy and excitement when I looked at it. It was all about how I wanted to feel in that series of Strictly Come Dancing *and what I wanted to achieve, so there were pictures that made me feel energized, happy and creative. I even drew a trophy and visualized holding it, imagining how good it would feel to have led a partner all the way to winning the final, knowing that I had accomplished my task successfully. However, I had not been specific enough. I put the vision board at the bottom of my cupboard and found it four months later, by which time I had come third in that series of* Strictly Come Dancing. *When I found the board, I realized I hadn't put a year on it, so I wrote 2008 next to the photo of the trophy and threw it back in the cupboard. Then 2008 was the year that Tom Chambers and I won. Of course it couldn't have happened just by visualizing it or writing it down; it took for me*

> 'First you imagine it, then you dream of it, then you take action and then you achieve it.'

to create routines, gain the audience's support and, of course, meet a partner who was capable and who had the same goal, but I'm convinced that the vision board played a big part too.

In 2011 I created a new vision board about becoming one of the judges on Strictly Come Dancing. *I wrote down how it would feel and what I would wear – I even cut out the judging panel from the show and stuck my picture on it! However, the picture I used was from the tour programme, not the TV show, and then in 2015 I was asked to be a judge on the tour!*

Before I wrote my first book, Strictly Inspirational, *I visualized a strong image of my husband cooking inside a house that we owned (at the time we were living in an apartment and had no deposit saved), and me in the garden writing my book. Then, five years later, that exact scenario happened! I also created a pretend book cover and wrapped it around one of the books on my shelf, so I would notice it every day when I was working in my office. I visualized what it would be like to see it in the bookstore for the first time and what it would feel like holding it in my hand. I can honestly tell you that actually holding the finished copy of my book in my hand was far more emotional than I ever imagined. I think mainly because writing in a second language wasn't something that I immediately thought I could do, so I achieved a big personal goal.*

EXERCISE 1: Visualization meditation

This simple meditation helps you to visualize yourself after your reinvention. Practise as often as you can until you have achieved your goal. The more you can visualize yourself after you have achieved your goal or reinvention, either by recalling an image or by imagining feeling a certain way, the more real the visualization will become and the more your mind will get used to feeling this way. This will help you to stay motivated to keep taking action toward it. This works in the same way as the law of attraction. You will attract more of what you focus on.

Although many people tell me they can't visualize, I know that with practice *anyone* can; even if you only hear sounds or are aware of feelings rather than seeing an actual image, it's still visualizing! It can help to enlist the help of a friend to talk you through the visualization – sharing your dreams with someone else helps to keep you accountable. Or you can head on over to my website where I've recorded an example of a visualization that you can listen to for free. Go to http://www.zenme.tv/reinventme/.

1. Sit somewhere comfortable where you won't be disturbed. Relax

with your eyes closed and take three deep breaths to allow you to be present in the moment. Then get ready to let your imagination flow.

2. Spend a few minutes focusing on your breath by imagining saying the word 'calm' on each in-breath, and the word 'relax' on each exhalation, until you notice every muscle in your body is relaxing. Literally imagine you are breathing calmness into each muscle.

3. Once you are fully relaxed, bring to mind an image of you after your reinvention, or bring to mind a sound or a feeling. Notice as many details as you can:

What are you wearing?

Where are you?

What sounds can you hear?

What are you doing?

Are you alone or with someone?

Pay attention to the emotions you are experiencing. Are you relaxed, happy, excited, proud? The more we can attach positive feelings to the visualization, the more the mind will believe it is achievable.

4. When you have a firm image or feeling, take three deep breaths in and as you exhale imagine you are exhaling positive energy into that vision or emotion. If you have a clear image, then turn up the colours in it and turn up the feelings too, just the way you would turn up the volume on the TV or radio. Then seal it with one more deep breath and open your eyes.

5. If a negative thought pops into your mind, then switch it for a positive one immediately. It's important to stick with making this a really positive experience for the mind.

6. Once you have done this and still with your eyes shut, imagine floating into the future above yourself, looking down onto your life and the timeline running through it and drop this visualization down into your future somewhere along the timeline at the exact date and year you would like to achieve your reinvention by. That way you are giving yourself a deadline too – most people get things done when they have a deadline.

Did you find it difficult to visualize? If so, don't worry. You may not get a strong image straight away – some people hear sounds or have strong feelings instead. Allow the visualization to come in whatever form is natural for you. There is no right or wrong way – there is just practising training your mind and allowing it to get used to this new way of imagining your future. In time visualization will become easier and feel more natural.

Sometimes a visualization is more like watching yourself in a movie – playing out what will happen, instead of seeing a single image. It can be helpful to imagine actually being in the movie so you are looking through your own eyes instead of observing from afar. Actually step into that screen and feel, see and hear everything as if it's happening for real.

EXERCISE 2: Making a vision board

This is hand on heart one of my favourite creative exercises to do for myself and with my clients, whether it's one-to-one or in a group. It's a great project to do with your partner or kids, too, for common goals.

Making vision boards really gets the creative flow going and as I mentioned in my story (see page 94) they have a magical way of working! You may want to make separate vision boards: for example, one for your personal goals, one for work and one for your love life. For now let's look at one for the reinvention you have been focusing on throughout this book.

1. Get a large piece of cardboard or use a journal if you prefer to be able to carry your visualization around with you.

2. Grab a pile of magazines, or search for images online, and find photos of yourself that reflect some of the emotions that you are trying to achieve. For example, if you are thriving to become more Zen, find photos of you relaxing. If your goal is to travel, find lots of photos representing the places you'd like to see or past photos of you on vacation. Rip out as many photos as you need from the magazines and add inspirational words and quotes that motivate and inspire you. Stick everything you've found on the board or in your journal. There are no right or wrong images or phrases, as long as they are positive ones – just choose whatever instinctively feels right and 'speaks' to you. Each time you look at your board, you should feel inspired and be able to imagine yourself once you've achieved your goal.

3. Put your creation where you will notice it. Or drop it in your cupboard like I did. We know it still worked, even from the bottom of my cupboard, because the intention had been set!

Were you surprised by what you discovered from your vision board? Is your reinvention goal clearer to you now?

Successful reinventions: Deborah, teacher

I knew it wasn't the greatest timing to break up with a long-term partner aged 36, especially given that I wanted to have children. However, that was not reason enough for me to stay in the relationship. There wasn't anything majorly wrong, but I had started making decisions that took me further away from my partner. I never thought twice about taking a job far from home, even one where I had to live in a different country. This seemed normal to me and I didn't really consider that it was not an ideal situation for him.

I suppose I should have noticed that my actions were speaking for themselves, but it wasn't until one day when I sat down in silence imagining and visualizing myself in the future that I realized that I couldn't see my partner in any of the images that came to my mind. I knew, in that moment, that deep down it was time to move on. I had a huge desire to travel and explore new things, but my partner was happiest at home with the dog. While I wanted to try new things, he felt more comfortable with what he knew. And although it's fine to do things apart as well as together in a relationship, I wanted something different for myself and I did not want to settle for something that was almost right. Of course the fearful thoughts set in: Will I fall in love again? Will I meet someone special in time to have children together? What will it be like to be single again at this age?

Even though I was the one who broke off the relationship, being single took some getting used to or rather it took my best friend to ask me, 'Are you going to sit there and feel sorry for yourself for much longer or are you going to get on the online dating and put yourself out there?' That was the kick in the butt I needed, my motivation if you like. Rather than just heading straight in, I started thinking about and visualizing my future partner – I felt that next time it would be even more important to ensure I'd found someone with all the qualities that were important to me. Then, reluctantly, I joined a few dating sites and, although I was single for a year, I met some really lovely men. Finally, I met my now husband and I had my first child when I was 42. I'm so glad that I held out for what I wanted, and that I didn't let the fear of being alone or running out of time to have children stand in the way of my happiness. I'm so grateful that I trusted what I'd seen in my visualization and took action to change what was in my power. Although what I did was scary and a gamble, it was one worth taking.

Overcoming barriers

I'm not entirely sure what I want to reinvent so how can visualization help me?

Even when you don't know what changes you want to make, using visualization allows you to connect with your intuition. You can do what I call a free-flow vision board, cutting out images that come to mind or that jump out at you from magazines. As you sit down to create, the images you choose may surprise you at first. I have worked with people who thought they wanted to buy a new house, but then made a vision board all about travelling. Making a vision board helped guide them toward what they actually wanted to do more than anything else. From that vision they could start taking action to make changes and fulfil their dreams. So I'd say to you just try some of the techniques in this chapter and be open-minded – who knows where it will take you?!

I'm so busy all the time. How often do I need to sit down and visualize?

Visualizing doesn't always have to be a big, scheduled task. Once you have practised a few times and created a strong image or feeling in your mind you can recall it anytime, even just for a couple of minutes. Visualizing can easily become part of your day if you just practise it little by little. For example, if you are dreaming of one day being the boss at work, every time you walk past the boardroom or your boss's office, take a moment to visualize what it would feel like to sit in that seat or be the chair of the boardroom meetings. Imagine what things you'd be dealing with. How would you dress? Would your posture be different? What would your day entail?

One friend of mine used visualization when she was going through the long process of IVF. She started with meditation, visualizing the eggs developing and being fertilized and then the embryo implanting and growing. Once she had these positive images in mind, she would recall them whenever she could – when going for a walk, while sitting on a train, just for a few minutes each day. She'd also visualize herself as a new mother, showing the baby to her neighbours and friends. I'm happy to say that, against all the odds, her IVF worked for her and she now has a wonderful little boy. How much the visualization helped she'll never know, but it certainly made the IVF process a more positive experience for her, which was really important.

Remember this ...

⟫ Creating a vision board physically and mentally helps to cement in your mind exactly what your vision is and gives focus and clarity on how to achieve your goal.

⟫ Other people may struggle to see your vision, but that does not mean it won't happen – that purely depends on your tenacity, passion and the action you take.

⟫ We have the power within us to turn our vision from fiction into reality when we visualize and take the necessary steps to make it happen.

'I imagine, I create, I live it.'

6.

EVOLVE

Definition: to gradually develop over a period of time into something different and usually more advanced.

Now, while I want you to stay positive about your reinvention – that new life or new you that you've visualized – I also want you to be realistic. Reinvention is unlikely to happen overnight – allowing yourself and your goal to evolve is a key part of the process. It will require patience, perseverance and a certain amount of flexibility. As I know from personal experience, reinvention isn't always a smooth path. Sometimes it can feel as if you're making your way out of a maze, while at other times it can be fun and exciting. You may have to adapt your plans, roll with the punches and to some extent let life happen.

As you try to evolve, you may meet resistance from those close to you and from yourself because of fear of the unknown and fear of change, especially if you are quite comfortable, albeit not content, as you are. But nothing ever stays exactly the same now does it? Life is constantly evolving, whether we want it to or not. If we want to create a fulfilled life for ourselves, the only real choice we have is to resist it or start evolving with it. Here's a good example of being passive and allowing life to evolve around you, or being proactive and taking charge of your own evolvement. Let's say you've been in a job for 10 years and that you've always been fairly ambitious, but you've become comfortable and reasonably content, so haven't bothered to do extra training, explore other areas within the business or evolved much on a personal level. Meanwhile, your colleague who is on a similar level has pushed himself that little bit further, learning new skills and taking a keener interest in the business overall, and evolved personally. When the business has to make cuts and choose between you, who do you think will be kept? Rather than being ready when the opportunity arose, life has evolved around you, leaving you no choice but to look for a new job. Having said that, sometimes that kind of push is exactly what we need to evolve, change and learn something new. How often have you heard someone say that being made redundant, although difficult at the time, turned out to be the best thing that happened to them?

I just want you to realize that there are different ways of evolving. You can decide to take charge of it yourself or you can wait until something happens or someone else decides for you – either way, we continually evolve. This can also be the case in relationships: perhaps you stayed with someone because it felt safe, even though you weren't happy, only to find further down the line your partner ended the relationship anyway, leaving you much more vulnerable than if you'd made that decision yourself, as well as perhaps feeling rejected and regretful.

I understand why it can be comfortable to stay as you are and choose not to evolve – it probably feels safer at the time and doing nothing is definitely less work and less immediate stress than making changes. It takes energy and curiosity to want to learn new things, especially as we get older, but trust me: to wait until you are pushed can take a lot more energy. Often we start playing it safe because, hey, if we haven't tried we haven't failed, right? WRONG – in my opinion, it's the *not* trying that is failing.

In order to evolve you have to allow yourself to make mistakes, to feel vulnerable sometimes and to have setbacks along the way. You have to allow for little hiccups in your plan and not allow them to stop you from moving forward. I'm yet to meet someone who has successfully reinvented themselves and not faced obstacles along the way. However, it's how they handled those obstacles that determined whether they succeeded or not. They saw the obstacles as challenges rather than stop signs or road blocks, learnt from them and proceeded.

It can be frustrating when you feel that you're starting all over again. There have been many times in my life when I have felt stupid because I knew so little about my new venture. Then I would remind myself that at least I had the courage to start a brand new journey and reassured myself that it was okay not to know everything overnight. With a smile to myself I would get over my embarrassment and think, well there's no time like the present to go ahead and study and learn whatever I need to.

At times when I have gone through personal reinvention, such as when I went through a very public relationship breakdown, I felt extremely vulnerable, as if the whole world was witnessing my change. What these experiences taught me is to accept what is and then make the most out of it. Evolving in a relationship can be hugely challenging at times because both partners need to change at the same speed, which rarely happens. It can teach us a lot about being patient with ourselves and with our partners. And it can teach us the huge lesson that just because we are evolving, we can't expect others to want to do the same. We can, however, lead the way and hope that they will follow, like shining the light but allowing them to find it when they are ready. It can be challenging to see someone you care about unhappy and it's difficult to allow them to be where they are at, and give them the space and time to come to their own realization, and it can be frustrating when they don't understand our need to evolve, but this is all part of you evolving personally.

Accepting you need to end a relationship in order to evolve can be one of the most difficult things of all. But the pain we go through, the difficult conversations we have, are all part of evolving. When we say goodbye to relationships, jobs and bad habits, we can start to rebuild ourselves, putting ourselves together in a new way, and become excited about all the new possibilities we have opened ourselves up to. Evolving isn't always easy, but I believe it is necessary.

MY STORY: Evolve

When I was aged 21 and still living in Denmark, I had a fabulous opportunity to continue being an estate agent after my apprenticeship had finished. Now, looking back over my life, I can't imagine what would have happened if I had done so. Not because of the job itself, but because by doing all the other jobs since, I have travelled the world, faced challenges, evolved and triumphed in a way I don't believe I would have if I had stayed put. Each challenge has taught me valuable lessons, which have helped me to evolve into a much more rounded and contented human being. Every job and relationship has helped me become more in touch with who I truly am.

I have walked away from well-paid jobs and ended relationships because they were no longer serving me or the other person. The older I got, the more I realized the consequences of my actions, knowing that my lifestyle would have to change and that I would have to sacrifice some luxuries for some time. I became more aware of the impact my decisions would have on my family and friends. I was aware I might fail, that I could suck at my new venture, that people might think I was foolish, and that I could lose my house and savings on something that didn't work out. And, yes, there were times when I didn't come out on top and I had to cut my losses more than once, but sometimes you just have to listen to yourself and understand deep within you what you want for yourself. How would you like to see yourself evolve? And then accept that if you are going to do those things, you may need to make massive changes and accept that there will be times of uncertainty.

A few years ago something very important about evolving suddenly came to me, like an epiphany. In 2013 I had gone back to Strictly Come Dancing *to be the assistant choreographer. The following year, having moved to LA and opened my Life Coaching business there, which was still in its infant stages in the US, I was asked to return to choreograph again. Although I had loved every minute, I knew deep down within me that choreographing was not my deepest desire – it wasn't my truth, my path. However much I loved working with the team, who were like family to me, I had no desire to create in that way any longer. So I sat down and had a long think about why I would potentially say yes and why I would say no. I considered how taking the job would help me to evolve. I realized that I would only take the job because I loved working with the team and would get paid a decent salary, but those were not good enough reasons and I couldn't see how doing the job would help my personal evolvement, which at that point in my life was very much at the top of my list of priorities – I felt I had learnt what I needed from that situation and I was craving to evolve in a different way.*

Then something else really important hit me. I realized that by taking the job I would, in fact, be blocking that space for someone who really wanted and needed to be there, someone whose creativity was waiting to be used in that way, someone who had a burning desire in their belly to be there. It was the same when I left the show as a professional dancer – by moving onto my journey, following my truth if you like, I had left a space open for someone else to evolve by stepping into the position I had left behind. This principle excited me because I started to imagine a world where we all move onto where we feel called to be without fear. When we allow the natural flow of evolvement, we can imagine someone else doing the same and leaving a space open for us.

Considering this when you are facing big choices can take away some of the fear. If we go against this natural flow, we not only block ourselves from experiences beyond what we can imagine but we also block someone else, and so the ripple effect continues.

In the same way, if you leave a relationship that isn't right for you, however hard that is, you are allowing yourself and your partner to go on to meet the right people. You leave space for the right relationships to evolve. When I wrote the email turning down the job, an email full of gratitude, I imagined someone else filling that space in a much better way. The job did in fact go to a dear friend of mine who needed to be in London much more than I did at that time, and it truly filled my heart to know that a greater plan had come together.

EXERCISE 1: Are you blocking your evolvement?

This exercise helps you to check in with yourself to make sure you are allowing your evolvement to flow freely and not blocking it in some subconscious way. Allow your answers to the questions below to guide you.

Ask yourself:
Am I blocking myself from flowing freely?

....

Am I blocking this space for someone else whose journey this is?

....

Am I holding a space that really is no longer in line with who I am?

....

Am I staying in a relationship or job for the wrong reasons and is it making me unhappy and stressed?

....

Ask yourself:
Is there space in my life to evolve?

....

How could I make some small changes that would allow there to be space for me to evolve?

....

Can you use what you've learnt to move on? For example, if you are single but working 24/7, how are you going to find time for a relationship? If you want to learn new skills, are you making time for evening courses? If getting fit and healthy is part of your reinvention, are you going to be able to have time for the gym or sports and still maintain your social schedule?

As you evolve it's important to understand what's in your power to change and what's not. Ask yourself:

What can I control?

....

What can't I control?

....

Do your answers make you feel more positive and empowered? For example, you can't control the demands that an employer or family or relationship makes, but you can control putting boundaries in place. You can't control that your workplace is halving its staff, but you can control how you react to it and what action you take to move on. You can't control that your partner has fallen out of love with you, but you can control how long you are going to dwell on it and decide whether you are going to keep carrying the sorrow into the future.

EXERCISE 2: Becoming more me

This is an exercise I love so much. Sometimes we are so busy running around being the perfect employee or boss, the perfect partner, the perfect parent, the perfect son or daughter, and so keen not to disappoint others that we disappoint ourselves. We don't go for that promotion because of family commitments; we don't go travelling the world because it's not the sensible thing to do according to xyz; we don't end a relationship because we don't want to hurt our partner. Just like that, you can ignore your deepest desires to evolve, ignore being true to yourself, or you can grab this opportunity and be honest with yourself as you have some fun answering these questions!

Becoming more me, means doing more of the following things ....

Becoming more me feels ....

Evolving to me means ....

Being true to who I am feels ....

How did it feel to put yourself first for a change? Great, I hope!

Successful reinventions: Suze, founder of Unplug Meditation

I was a fashion editor with a busy schedule and a family. Life was good but stressful, so my mother-in-law suggested that I take up meditation. I took her advice and was soon aware of the many benefits, but I wanted a place to meditate without having to do the yoga – like a dry bar for meditation. I couldn't find that anywhere, so I thought, 'How about creating one! Surely I wasn't the only person who just wanted to go and meditate?'

I had no idea how I would achieve this goal. I knew all about being a fashion editor, but nothing about running a business. However, I was open to learning and passionate about my project. I quickly found that you learn by going through the experience yourself. I thought it was frustrating at times that people couldn't just tell me what they knew, but I know now that I had to learn in order to grow and be in charge of my vision.

I have definitely evolved as a business person and on a personal level through this process. I learnt, for example, that impatience didn't get things done and that motivating your staff with kind words and support worked much better. I also learnt that I don't always have to react to something immediately – it's okay to take my time to respond. One of the biggest lessons I would like to share is that even taking baby steps each day will help get you there.

Of course it didn't all just happen; I had many moments of fear and doubt. I remember one day crying and telling a close friend that I wasn't sure how to make this happen, that it felt too hard and that a lot of people were saying it wasn't going to work. She took my hand and said, 'I believe in you' and that was all the support I needed. From then on I literally imagined putting all my fears, which were blocking me, in an imaginary box and putting it under an imaginary bed and that's where they have stayed ever since. With the fear put aside, I got on with taking action.

When you have a dream, it's okay to let it evolve gradually; it doesn't have to be an abrupt ending. For example, if necessary, hold on to your day job and slowly explore the new area you're interested in. There are many resources and courses online, which are hugely beneficial when taking on a new challenge. Don't get bogged down in the detail: I didn't ever waste my time on the how, but instead focused on what I could do every day and task by task I got there. One of the most helpful tools we have at the studio is a suggestion box – the comments from clients are vital as I'm fully aware that I'm learning and evolving every single day.

'Just an hour of focused attention a day, if that's all the time you have, can bring you closer to your reinvention.'

Overcoming barriers

My plans to retrain have been put on hold for financial reasons. I can't see a way back now.

Often finances can stand in the way or be an excuse we use not to commit to our reinvention. I believe there is always a way, even if it's not obvious at first. While at a dinner party recently someone was telling me how they were curious about learning more about positive psychology, but that they weren't sure they could invest the money to train. Then the lady who was sitting next to me blurted out, 'I'll teach you.' Just like that, a connection was made. The action this person took was to say, 'I need help. Can anyone help me?' If finances are tight, tap into everything that's available to you.

There is so much free information and so many courses online and people who want to help or swap skills. I have often taught someone a subject I'm an expert in and in return they have taught me something – a win-win situation. Cast your net wide, on social media, by talking to friends, or even to strangers, at the gym for example. What is there to lose by asking? Instead of thinking it can't happen, think 'How can I make this happen?' I know many people who were curious about working in the theatre or the fitness business and so they started by volunteering in that field and ended up as permanent staff, loving their job and life.

I love my partner, but I feel like I'll never fully evolve and be true to myself while I'm with him. What should I do?

Narrow down what is making you feel this way and then start communicating with your partner. Sometimes our partners reflect back to us things we need to work on and heal within, and sometimes they reflect things we have already gone through. It's important to know which of the two it is.

If you have always been a fixer (someone who enjoys the challenge of fixing someone else) in a relationship, you may no longer want to play that role. You need to be honest and say I'm done 'fixing', I need you to step up and make changes too. Not communicating how we feel, hoping things will work themselves out, is a huge reason why things go wrong in relationships. Communication in a relaxed and open manner where both parties listen and speak is key. If this is not possible, consider seeking help from someone neutral such as a Life Coach or therapist.

Making changes can feel like being at sea in stormy weather, but once our personal changes settle, the relationship may fall into place. Being patient is key. When someone in a relationship asks me, 'Do you think we are right for each other?', my reply is always, 'What do you think? If you are asking that question, maybe you need to have a big think about your relationship. Would you want to be in a relationship where your partner is asking this question about you? Or do you want to be in a relationship where you just know and they know that it's right?

Remember this ...

⟩ Be patient with yourself as you evolve. Know that no matter how confusing it can be, there will eventually be clarity if you trust in your own ability.

⟩ There are no mistakes. It's all part of getting us where we need to get so we can learn what we need to learn.

⟩ Trust that you are exactly where you need to be at this stage of your life and that you are on the right path, even when it feels like a detour.

'I am committed to evolving,
changing and growing so that
I can be the best version
of myself and bring my light
to this world.'

'I am a creative and beautiful
human being and I have all that
I need within me.'

7.
NURTURE

Definition: To nourish and support.

Nurturing is a crucial part of this reinvention programme, both nurturing your talents and yourself. Going through any type of change requires energy, commitment and perseverance, so it's essential to look after both body and mind.

I have learnt what it truly means to nurture from personal experience and from the many clients I have had the honour of working with over the years. Many have had a thriving business yet felt at an all-time low in their personal lives, and vice versa – I have seen clients dedicated to raising a family to the point where they have nothing left to give at work or to themselves. When we are flying high in one area of our lives, it's easy to keep our focus on that and neglect other areas. For example, you might work really long hours because you enjoy it or because you accept it as the price you have to pay for regular promotions and salary increases, but as a result you tend to eat on the go, have no time for exercise, feel stressed, have no time for a relationship or a social life or any other creative outlets that would help nurture your talents. When this is the case, you might find you wake up one day feeling totally exhausted physically and mentally.

There's nothing wrong with deciding to dedicate, say, a couple of months or even a few years to a new project where you give it your full attention, but it is another thing to fall into a pattern where this is just how it is all the time and taking care of yourself comes way down on your list of priorities. This is not sustainable in the long run – we are not machines and if we don't eat well, exercise and rest enough it will take its toll on us. In my opinion, nurturing should be at the top of your list of priorities, however busy you are. I personally schedule in lie-ins, massages or hot baths – just a little 'me time' – because I know that is what I need in order to be my happy self. When I start to neglect those things, I become someone who I'm not and who I don't like – frustrated, stressed and moody. When I started to consider how to nurture all areas of my life, the word that came to mind was balance.

Knowing yourself and saying 'this is what I need to be the best version of myself' may mean a change of outlook and take some getting used to, but it's essential. Nobody else can do this for you and when you are run down and exhausted and have nothing to give it will be too late, the flu will have set in or you will have snapped at someone or even worse hit rock-bottom exhaustion. At that point you are not doing yourself or the people around you any favours. We need to learn to notice the signs before it comes to this. I know you might be thinking, 'But I'm so busy I simply haven't got the time for this.' I understand that concern, I have been there many times and it took me a complete creative and personal burnout to realize, but knowing what I know now, it's all a matter of prioritizing at all times what is truly most important to us. We have to monitor ourselves by raising our awareness.

The other equally important part of nurture is nurturing your talents and creative outlets. When you feel as if you are running on empty, doing something creative that uses your talents can inspire you and fuel other areas of your life. The magical thing that happens when you nurture your talents is that you tap into something creative – the child within, if you like – and by doing so you allow yourself to be fully immersed in that thing. For example, let's say you like drawing – when you are doing that, you are fully present, concentrating only on this skill. It's meditative, which allows your mind to take a rest from its usual concerns and stresses. Once you have finished, you feel refreshed and then carry this positive feeling into other areas of your life. When dancing was my hobby, before it became my profession, I would finish my day job and sometimes arrive at practice feeling majorly stressed. However, by the time I finished my practice I felt energized and had completely forgotten what I was stressed about.

When you nurture the different skills and talents that you have, you may even find ways to interlink your skills to build a bridge between the two. For example, I was doing Life Coaching long before I made it my main business. I used to coach people

I would meet through dancing, TV and theatre so I was able to nurture that skill alongside my other work. The exercises in this chapter help you to look at all aspects of your life to ensure you have the right balance between creating and resting, work and fun.

MY STORY: **Nurture**

When I was working really hard to get to the top of my game in competitive ballroom dancing, I was undoubtedly nurturing my passion for performing and dancing. However, I worked so hard that I forgot to nurture my body in the way it needed and deserved. I wanted to succeed so badly and for all the hard work to pay off now. I was convinced that if I took my foot of the pedal for one second by having a day of rest or allowing myself a bit of pampering, that someone else would reach that goal before me. Even when I did take a day off, I was not present and enjoying it; instead my thoughts would still be racing at 100 miles an hour, thinking about the routine I was working on at the time and worrying that I wasn't in the studio rehearsing. So it wasn't really rest at all, it was just more work.

This wasn't a very healthy approach and definitely not one that nurtured me physically and mentally in the best way. The result was that my immune system was often weak and I would catch every cold going, and because my body was fatigued it was easy to pull muscles and get minor injuries. I wasn't making time to wind down properly, so I often felt stressed, tired and snappy, which meant I wasn't firing on all cylinders when I really needed to get ahead in competitions. It took me to hit a complete burnout to realize I had to make changes in my life and start to nurture myself, but it doesn't have to get to that place for you.

Once I started incorporating mindful practices into my life, for example being more mindful of what I ate and how I exercised, and taking time to have regular massages, things improved. Nowadays if I have a busy day coaching, it is simply a priority for me to make sure I have eaten right and exercised, even if I've only had time to go for a walk. Eating the right food, having the right amount of sleep and scheduling in a power nap or a 5-minute meditation is part of my life. I have realized I have to prepare according to my schedule and having balance has become my main priority. It means that there is balance between creating and resting, teaching and learning, using energy and filling myself up. Nowadays, knowing what a burnout feels like, I notice the warning signs before it's too late and I make sure I take action before it gets to that.

'Be mindful of your thoughts as they have the power to become your reality.'

EXERCISE 2: Meditation – 'Energy follows thought'

This wonderful meditation, one of my favourites, helps you work out where you should be focusing your energy.

In my mid-twenties I was feeling frustrated and wondering if I would ever achieve my dancing goals, and I seriously considered giving up on my dream. Then a very special woman told me three very important words that changed my life – 'Energy follows thought'. She encouraged me to put these words on the wall where I could look at them every day and to be mindful of what I spent my energy on, especially my 'mental energy' – my thoughts. I realized quite quickly that I used a lot of energy worrying about what my competitors were doing, comparing myself to them and their journey and feeling frustrated that I wasn't getting the gigs they were getting or mastering a step the way they did. I soon became mindful of all the energy I was wasting thinking about things that were out of my control and which had nothing to do with my journey. I started to catch myself whenever my thoughts would go there and redirect my energy back to myself. I'd ask myself where is my energy best spent for me to improve and nurture my talents? One of the biggest revelations was how much time I suddenly had now that I was only focusing on and nurturing myself and how much more clarity of mind I had. It was powerful and my career and life from that moment went from strength to strength.

Of course it's human to get caught up in other people's lives, especially when we pick up a magazine or read a social media post. But having this little tool in our back pockets means that we can switch our thinking, redirect our energy as soon as we notice and instead of being envious of someone, feel inspired: think instead 'I can't wait to do that myself' or 'If they can do it, so can I.'

So write down those words – 'Energy follows thought' – where you can see them, then try this meditation to work out where you are spending your energy and whether you need to switch it to somewhere else. Have your notebook to hand in case helpful thoughts come to mind that you want to write down after you have done the meditation.

Sit comfortably somewhere you can relax and close your eyes.

As you breathe in each time, relax each part of your body from the tip of your toes to the top of your head until you feel completely relaxed in your entire body.

Then just sit there quietly noticing your breath and bring your focus onto the question: 'Where am I directing my energy in my life?' What am I giving my attention to? Then just sit with that question for a moment and you may notice that different helpful thoughts pop into your mind. Just allow for them to come, they may come while you meditate or later, either way is fine.

Then after a few minutes, change it to the following thought: 'Do I need to redirect my energy so that it can be spent in a more beneficial way to me?'

And finally. 'Where shall I direct my energy, attention and focus so that it is nurturing my reinvention?'

After a few minutes, open your eyes and jot down anything that came to mind.

Take a moment to consider consciously where you would like to direct your energy. What would you like to give your attention to? Write it down.

EXERCISE 2: Detoxing your lifestyle

When you're nurturing yourself and your talents, consider if your lifestyle is in line with what you are trying to achieve. When we think about detoxing, we usually focus on our diet. For this exercise, I want you to take detoxing to a new level and consider if there is anything else in your life you need to detox to bring your lifestyle in alignment with your reinvention?

For example, if you are working on getting over a relationship and trying to find happiness again, consider what type of music you listen to, what TV shows you watch and how you talk about your situation to others. If you listen to sad songs and watch depressing movies about relationships not working out, these will evoke negative feelings and will not help you toward healing. If you swap to more positive music, TV and movies, they will put you in a different mindset and slowly you will shift your perception. It's okay to feel the sadness of something, but there comes a point when it's time to take action and move on.

Another area to detox may be a friend who is negative and drains you, or who isn't supportive of your reinvention efforts. Or perhaps your house is so cluttered that there is no space for you to feel inspired and creative. All of these things combined, as well as diet and exercise, can either support or hinder your journey.

So, I ask you now to become mindful of who you surround yourself with, what you listen to, what you watch, the words you use and everything else you spend your precious energy on. Take a moment here to consider what you need to detox to allow your lifestyle to support your reinvention in the best possible way?

Music: ....

Home: ....

TV shows: ....

Food: ....

Friends: ....

Body: ....

Look at your answers and start making small changes. It doesn't have to be an overnight detox. Once you change one area, other more positive life choices will naturally follow.

EXERCISE 3: Nurture goal chart

Fill out a chart with suggestions of things that you would like to bring into your life that would help you to nurture yourself more:

My mind: Write down those things that would help you relax: for example, a daily or weekly nature walk, a daily 5-minute meditation, reading a book for 20 minutes each day.

My talents: For example, if you love writing, you could start a blog. If you danced as a teenager, you could take up dancing again now. If you have a talent for computer programming, you could start an online course in web developing. If you love baking, you could set up a small sideline baking cakes. By nurturing talents such as these, you might at the same time earn money and ultimately start on the path that will lead you to where you want to go.

My body: Write down foods that would nurture you, and specific vegetables and fruits that you would like to introduce into your life. Write down healthy swaps, such as dates instead of chocolate, raw carrots instead of crisps. If you want to exercise more, set yourself a goal of what you'd like to achieve, whether that's walking or running a certain distance, or attending a particular gym class. Feeling healthier in body and mind will help you to feel strong within and help you find the confidence to follow your dreams.

Do these changes seem more achievable now that they're written down? It can be rewarding to tick them off as and when you achieve them.

Successful reinventions: Joanne, businesswoman

I was a CEO of a successful company, divorced and single, eating out and partying in posh clubs in London most nights and getting VIP treatment, which often meant hanging out with celebrities. I was definitely flying high and to most people my life appeared to be glamorous. It was fun for a while, but my stress levels at work were at an all-time high and burning the candle at both ends was starting to take its toll on my body and my health in a big way.

I wasn't feeling well and I had put on a lot of weight from drinking too much alcohol and from constantly eating the wrong things on the go, so much so that I didn't recognize myself when I looked in the mirror any more. I used to be very health conscious and nurture myself, but I had got sucked into my job and the lifestyle that came with it.

Two things happened that made me stop in my tracks, re-evaluate my life and realize it was time for reinvention. One night at home my teenage daughter confronted me with the words, 'Mum I wish you would stop drinking so much, it's not good for your health and I'm worried about you.' This really hit home immediately. I didn't see myself as someone who had an addiction or a problem with alcohol; just someone who looked to enjoy life. I was surprised that she had noticed it, but as I sat there shocked by her comment, digesting my daughter's words, I realized that drinking alcohol had become part of my routine. The more I went for boozy lunches and dinners, the less I did anything to nurture myself and to ease my stress – quite the opposite in fact, I had let myself go.

Not long after this conversation I remember sitting around a dinner table with a bunch of people I hardly knew, thinking what on earth am I doing to myself, this is not who I am. That really was a defining moment. A few days later I decided to open up to a friend about my situation and she suggested that I went to an AA meeting. It was tough, I was in denial for a while as to how bad the social drinking had become, there were lots of tears and a lot of resistance from me before I started making any changes, but I kept thinking of the impact that me not nurturing myself would have on my daughter and that became my motivation.

It took time to realize and accept that although I by no means drank from morning to night, I had created an unhealthy lifestyle for myself. Step by step I started to make small nurturing changes to my life. It was like I was finding my way back to who I truly was. My health also improved and I started exercising again. I began to make different choices in my life, such as meeting with a friend and heading to yoga and catching up over a green tea instead of going to a bar. It took a year until I really felt like I had my health and body back on track and before the stress at work had subsided too. Making these conscious nurturing choices in my life meant I suddenly felt so much more focused in my life and like I had so much more clarity and energy for myself, my family and my work.

'You see your reflection in other people. If you no longer recognize what you see, then tune in and figure out a way to change that reflection.'

Overcoming barriers

I've heard that meditation helps with anxiety and stress, but how can I warrant sitting still when I have a million things to do?!

I can totally relate to this question. I was someone who used to drive through life in fifth gear, thinking that sitting still would slow me down rather than help propel me forward. I have to admit to you that I was wrong. Now, no matter how busy I am, I find a few minutes to connect to my breath before I leave the house in the morning. I simply don't have the time not to meditate, because when I have meditated in the morning everything else goes just that little bit smoother for the rest of the day. For example, I'm less likely to get frustrated when I'm stuck in traffic or if someone is rude to me; instead I feel like I have this inner patience with myself and others that overflows into everything I do. Meditation makes it easier to stay focused on one thing at a time and be more present in each thing that you do, whether you are working or busy at home.

Meditating can be as simple as sitting still and counting your breath – in 1, out 2, in 3, out 4 – up to 20. Or you can use words like 'relax' as you breathe in and 'now' as you exhale; just repeating those words to yourself, noticing your breath going all the way down into your belly and out. You can even do that with your eyes open if you have to. I have literally used this exercise in situations that needed calming down while looking directly at people, and it's powerful to notice that by relaxing you have an effect on the people around you. Making this connection with yourself at the beginning of the day is magical and it's something that I wish every person in the world would do. When it's possible, repeat the exercise later in the day too. I can almost guarantee you that once you introduce mindful meditation into your day it will become a habit you will want to keep for life and you will probably wonder just the way I have, why you didn't introduce it sooner!

My husband isn't happy about me spending so much time with my new choir, but I love singing so much – it makes me feel happy and alive. What should I do?

I hear this situation a lot from my clients, when a partner or family member is bothered by them spending a lot of time on their hobby. Perhaps your husband doesn't realize how much being in the choir means to you, so try to communicate this. Try to get him to see the advantages of you enjoying this hobby, such as you being happier and having more energy and therefore being a nicer person to live with.

One of the most beautiful things we can do for another person is to allow them to be who they are and allow them space to grow and evolve. It seems difficult to understand why someone would deny a person the happiness of doing what they love, so try to find out what's at the root of your husband's concerns. It could be that he feels he doesn't see you enough.

If so, perhaps you can find a balance that works for both of you. Perhaps you can find a compromise where you can still practise your singing but be home more. Or is there a way you can involve your husband in your hobby?

Sometimes loved ones might worry about us branching out because of the people we might meet and the separate life we will have, and this may trigger an insecurity within them. In this case it helps to reassure the other person – although their insecurity is something that person needs to heal themselves, you can still be sensitive to it. If your husband doesn't have a change of heart, consider the consequences of continuing with your hobby and what you are willing to risk in order to pursue it. Writing down the pros and cons of attending the choir may help, then you can weigh everything up and work out what needs to happen.

There is also the possibility that this problem is the symptom of a bigger underlying issue that needs clearing up and working on so that there is room for both of you to be who you truly are.

Remember this ...

⟩ When you take the time to nurture yourself, it's a long-term investment you will not regret. Even nurturing a talent or passion that may never become more than that, may be exactly what needs to happen to spark something within and lead you toward the right path and the true you.

⟩ When you open up to noticing all the possibilities within and around you, blockages disappear and fear is replaced with excitement and curiosity.

⟩ Meditating for just five minutes a day can make a huge difference and you will find clarity and focus where before you felt confused and overwhelmed.

'I make healthy choices for my body and mind so I can be the best version of myself.'

'I make nurturing my talents and myself a priority and I always find time for it.'

'I decide where I direct my energy and I have the power to redirect it at any time.'

8.

TRANSFORMATION

Definition: A change or alteration, especially a radical one.

Well done! You have made it to the last chapter of the book. You have all the tools necessary for your transformation, for turning your dreams into a reality.

Good job for hanging in there, finding the courage to be so honest with yourself, and committing to doing the exercises and making all the positive changes necessary for your reinvention. By now you should have your first step of action written down. If you haven't, take a moment to do that now.

I have written some of the exercises in the checklist opposite for you as a reminder, just in case you left any out. You may want to have a quick flick through the book or your notes. Also know that at any point you can come back to one of the chapters and redo any of the exercises as you evolve with your reinvention or perhaps as you reinvent one thing you find something else you want to reinvent. Exercises such as the vision board (see pages 100–101) and the 'energy follows thought' meditation (see pages 134–6) are helpful ones to keep using as they will change and evolve with you.

Checklist of exercises

RECOGNIZE
1. Who am I? ☐
2. Identify ☐
3. Before and after ☐

EGO
1. What is truly important to you? ☐
2. Ego-buster ☐
3. Does your ego define you? ☐
4. Are you ready to set yourself free? ☐

INNOVATION
1. Making a plan ☐
2. Meditation – 'Planting the seeds in the garden of opportunity' ☐

NOW
1. Now is the time ☐
2. Fear-buster map ☐
3. Letting go ☐
4. Be present meditation ☐

VISUALIZE
1. Visualization meditation ☐
2. Making a vision board ☐

EVOLVE
1. Are you blocking your evolvement? ☐
2. Becoming more me ☐

NURTURE
1. Meditation – 'Energy follows thought' ☐
2. Detoxing your lifestyle ☐
3. Nurture goal chart ☐

Contract with myself

Writing things down is one thing and sticking to the plan is another, so I have created a contract for you below. This is your time to make a contract with yourself, to commit to putting into action all of the preparation you have done throughout this book. This will make your goal more real and you will know you have committed to following it through. Because just like training for a marathon you have to do the practice, but you also have to show up on race day to get the medal. You can create your own contract if you want to make it even more personal to you.

I .... commit to making positive changes to support me and create space in my life for my reinvention. I am committed to taking daily, weekly and monthly action toward my goal. I'm excited and I believe in myself and my ability to achieve this. I feel supported and I am ready.

You may want to keep your reinvention plans private, but if not it can help to let a partner or friend know of your commitment. They can help to keep you accountable and maybe you can support them in their reinvention. I, for example, started telling people I was finishing my book, so I knew I would do it long before the deadline. I also committed to creating my website by buying the domain name and putting up a holding page saying 'coming soon' to make a contract with myself. Keeping yourself accountable and creating deadlines will help you stick to your plan. I promise you there are projects vital to my reinvention that I would have never done had I not asked for or created my own deadlines. We are all capable of amazing things once we fully commit ourselves.

Final thoughts

When we embark on new journeys we may feel vulnerable at times and we may stumble, but remember that many people have gone before you and succeeded, overcoming huge hurdles. Know that the difference between you achieving or not achieving your goal can be as simple as you believing you can do it and you believing that you can't, or the difference between someone who fell and gave up and someone who got up, carried on and succeeded.

I believe in you and I respect you for committing to changing something in your life, so that you can be a happier and more contented person. I have let you know that I have felt vulnerable many times in my life and I have had moments of OMG, how is this going to actually come together, but I kept walking forward, I committed fully and I kept my eye on the goal. Sometimes we have to detour to get to where we need to be and that's fine too. Have faith in yourself and know that you are far more powerful and capable than you probably give yourself credit for. And remember it's okay to ask for help when we need it. I wish for you to live your life the way it was meant to be lived, to its fullest potential. You didn't come here to play it small, you came here to shine your light so bright that everyone can see it.

I want to leave you with just one more question:

What is the deepest reason for your reinvention and how will your reinvention positively impact the world around you?

PS ...
Imagine if everything you are searching for outside of yourself is already within you.

FURTHER READING

Bernstein, Gabrielle, *Spirit Junkie Harmony and Miracles Now* (both Hay House)
This author has a funky young way about her, which is very engaging. *Spirit Junkie* is a great introduction to motivational self-help books. She also teaches a course in miracles from her perspective. I became aware and now practice kundalini yoga thanks to her recommendation.

Branson, Richard, *Losing My Virginity* (Virgin Publishing)
I read this a long time ago. My favourite part of the book is where Richard talks about starting out and how he never lost his self-belief. He never gave up – even when all the banks said no, he knew one would say yes.

Brown, Brené, *The Gifts of Imperfection* (Hazelden)
This book is so helpful in reminding us how we should all be kind to ourselves.

Byrne, Rhonda, *The Magic* and *The Secret* (both Atria Books)
What I love about these books is that they sum up so many great ideas in a very easy straightforward way.

Chopra, Deepak, *The Seven Spiritual Laws of Success*
(Bantam Press)
>A wonderful straightforward book that guides you to a
deeper spiritual understanding. It's very helpful to practise
these seven laws, especially the law of detachment.

Davidji, *Secrets of Meditation* (Hay House)
>I love Davidji's relaxed way of explaining the depths of
meditation. He has such a charming, fun and warm way of
explaining the benefits and tools both in person and in the
written word. If you have questions about meditation or are
curious about starting or deepening your journey, this book
is very helpful.

Ferriss, Timothy, *The 4-Hour Work Week* (Barnes & Noble)
>This is what I call 'how to work smart'. I love this book, and
it helped me hugely in my time management.

Foundation for Inner Peace, *A Course in Miracles*
>I recommend doing the exercises in this book if you are
going through a tough time, and are searching for a deep
spiritual text to find self-love.

Hay, Louise, *You Can Heal Your Life* (Hay House)
My 'go-to' book – I love the affirmations and suggestions she gives. Her life story is fascinating, and Louise is a huge inspiration to me. I refer to this book for all causes. It describes how different emotions can be linked to different diseases. This book comes with me whenever I travel.

Keller, Gary W. & Papasan, Jay, *The One Thing* (John Murray Learning)
This book is a bestseller for a reason, because it's excellent! It hammers home the importance of focusing on one thing and reminds you to figure out what is your one thing!

McKenna, Paul, *Instant Confidence* (Bantam Press)
This was my go-to book, mostly on repeat, when I was feeling low.

Massey, Alexandra, *Beat Depression Fast* (Watkins)
This story I love because the author describes so honestly how she found her way out of a depression – not by using drugs, but by self-discovery and using the exercises described in this wonderful book.

O'Connor, Joseph, *NLP Workbook* (HarperCollins)
This book helped me greatly when I was studying Neuro-Linguistic Programming (NLP).

Redfield, James, *The Celestine Prophecy* (Grand Central Publishing)
This book was vital in my career. It has taught me to stay open-minded when I meet new people, and not be afraid to ask, talk and share information.

Robbins, Anthony, *Awaken the Giant Within* (Simon & Schuster)
This was an empowering read when I needed it most. Anthony Robbins always speaks with such authority – I find that engaging in itself.

Spackman, Dr Kerry, *The Winner's Bible* (HarperCollins)
I love this – everyone should create a winner's bible for themselves.

Tad, James & Woodsmall, Wyatt, *Time Line Therapy* (Meta Publications)
I find the concept of Time Line Therapy very helpful in understanding and getting to the root cause of an issue.

Tolle, Eckhart, *The Power of Now* (New World Library) and
A New Earth (Penguin)
There were such wonderful messages in these books. I
refer to them often when I get pulled off track and want
reminding of how to live in the now.

Virtue, Doreen, *Chakra Clearing* (audio) (Hay House)
I love this audio, especially if I have been surrounded by lots
of people or negativity. It helps me feel centred and cleansed.

Virtue, Doreen, *The Lightworker's Way* (Hay House)
Beautiful story about how Doreen started out.

Winfrey, Oprah, *What I Know For Sure* (Macmillan)
I call this the 'little book of wisdom'. I use daily Oprah's
advice that before taking on anything she asks herself 'Do
I have a burning desire for this?' and, if not, she says no.

Williamson, Marianne, *A Return to Love* (HarperCollins)
To me Marianne is the queen bee of inspirational speakers.
I go to listen to her live as much as possible when I'm in LA.
She teaches the principles of 'A Course in Miracles', which
is quite a heavy text to read at first, which I why I love this
book – it describes the principles in a more accessible way.

ABOUT THE AUTHOR

SACRE IMAGES

Camilla Sacre-Dallerup is an author, Life Coach and Mindful Living Expert. She is a NLP master practitioner, certified hypnotherapist and a popular meditation teacher at Unplug Meditation and The Den in LA. She is the founder and head coach of www.Zenme.tv (see overleaf). Camilla is a motivational speaker and holds workshops in the UK and US, including 'Design Your Ideal Partner', 'Reinvent Me' and 'Forgive and Set Yourself Free'.

Camilla was a successful competitive athlete in ballroom dancing for 25 years and was part of the original cast of *Strictly Come Dancing* (UK's equivalent of *Dancing With the Stars*), which she won in 2008. Camilla is passionate about sharing what she has learnt as a top athlete and by being in the media spotlight. Her mission is to help others succeed using the tools that have helped her, such as Neuro-Linguistic Programming (NLP), hypnosis, meditation and mindfulness, and to inspire people to meditate and take time for self-care daily.

Her highly acclaimed first book, *Strictly Inspirational*, was published in 2015. This is her second book. Camilla lives in LA with her husband Kevin and their dogs.

About Zenme

Zenme is a mindful community and coaching, meditation and hypnosis business based in Los Angeles and Camilla is the founder and head coach. Using all of the skills and tools she has accumulated through her time as an athlete and Life and Mindful Living Expert, along with what she learnt through her training in coaching and hypnosis, the tools used at Zenme vary, depending on the needs of the client, but include meditation, NLP (Neuro-Linguistic Programming), hypnosis, mindful living practices and many more. Go to www.zenme.tv for more information.

Camilla would love to hear about your reinvention and how this book has supported you.
To connect with Camilla go to

    www.facebook.com/CamillaDallerup

    twitter @camilladallerup

    instagram @camilladallerup

Sign up for her newsletter on www.zenme.tv to stay up-to-date and receive news about workshops and free meditations.

journal pages
